Questioning the Veil

Questioning the Veil

Open Letters to Muslim Women

Marnia Lazreg

HQ
1170
.L39
2009

Princeton University Press
Princeton and Oxford

Copyright © 2009 by Princeton University Press
Published by Princeton University Press, 41 William Street, Princeton,
New Jersey 08540
In the United Kingdom: Princeton University Press, 6 Oxford Street,
Woodstock, Oxfordshire OX20 1TW

Library of Congress Cataloging-in-Publication Data

Lazreg, Marnia.
Questioning the veil : open letters to Muslim women / Marnia Lazreg.
p. cm.
Includes bibliographical references and index.
ISBN 978-0-691-13818-3 (hbk. : alk. paper) 1. Muslim women.
2. Hijab (Islamic clothing) 3. Veils—Religious aspects—Islam. I. Title.
HQ1170.L39 2009
297.5'76—dc22
2009003499

British Library Cataloging-in-Publication Data is available

This book has been composed in Adobe Caslon Pro

Printed on acid-free paper. ∞

press.princeton.edu
Printed in the United States of America
3 5 7 9 10 8 6 4

*In gratitude to the memory of my mother,
whose openness on the world and indomitable will to
freedom nurtured me and continue to inspire me.*

We are not [wo]men for whom it is a question of "either-or." For us, the problem is not to make a utopian and sterile attempt to repeat the past, but go beyond it.

—Aimé Césaire, *Discourse on Colonialism*

Contents

Acknowledgments

WRITING THESE LETTERS was not an easy task: it required me to say things I normally would not have said about issues that had troubled me in the past but which I let alone with the hope that they might just come to pass. But they have not, and facing them meant facing myself, drawing on bits and pieces of my life to explain myself at the risk of whittling away at that special zone of privacy that I treasure so much. However, there are situations when commitment to change makes it incumbent on the writer to reveal herself as a person and put down the theoretical and methodological shields that usually ensure a semblance of detachment. I offer these letters in a spirit of candor.

I deeply appreciate the trust that all the women I interviewed placed in me by sharing with me their thoughts and feelings. I have reproduced their words with accuracy, and I hope that my interpretation of their experiences is helpful to them and will contribute to a better understanding of the issue of veiling. I must also thank Sondra Hale for taking the time to read the manuscript and for her incisive comments.

I have a special debt of gratitude toward my editor, Brigitta Van Rheinberg, who was receptive to the idea of writing these letters, encouraged it, and supported it. I could not have completed this project without her sustained commitment and dedication.

A number of people helped in researching the relevant materials. Akim Oualhaci's superb research skills were immensely useful in making sense of the headscarf controversy in France, and understanding the French construction of Muslim identity. Louisa Rachel Khettab volunteered her time to scour bibliographical sources. Jean-Jacques Strayer at the Jacqueline Wexler Library (Hunter College) was always ready to provide expert assistance whenever I needed it. Last but not least, Curtis Matthew, head of the Circulation Department, Mina Rees Library (Graduate Center of the City University of New York), gave me access to precious sources in a period of crunch. I cannot thank him enough for his generosity and diligence.

Questioning the Veil

Introduction

IN MY PREVIOUSLY PUBLISHED WORK, I have consistently objected to the manner in which Muslim women have been portrayed in books as well as the media. On the one hand, they have been represented as oppressed by their religion, typically understood as being fundamentally inimical to women's social progress. From this perspective, the veil has traditionally been discussed as the most tangible sign of women's "oppression." On the other hand, Muslim women have been described as the weakest link in Muslim societies, which should be targeted for political propaganda aimed at killing two birds with one stone: showing that Islam is a backward and misogynous religion, and underscoring the callousness or cruelty of the men who use Islam for political aims. Such a view made it acceptable to hail the war launched against Afghanistan in 2001 as a war of "liberation" of women. Subsequently, the American-sponsored constitutions of both Afghanistan and Iraq were lauded as protecting the "rights" of women in spite of evidence to the contrary.[1] In this context, any Muslim woman who takes cheap shots at Islam and crudely indicts Muslim cultures is perceived as speaking the truth and is elevated to stardom.

I do not wish to enter the fray on one side or the other of the ideological struggle for or against Islam. I have no animus against Islam. I was born to a Muslim family in a predominantly Muslim country, and I am proud of my heritage. I have decided to write these letters to women whose religion is Islam and who either have taken up the veil or are thinking of wearing it. However, writing about women necessarily means writing about men. To many in the Muslim world, well-meaning individuals beleaguered by geopolitical events, these letters may seem pointless. But perhaps such individuals need to resolve the apparently unimportant issue of veiling before they can defend themselves more effectively. These letters are also relevant to all people, women and men, seeking to understand the human experience. I have reached a point in my life when I can no longer keep quiet about an issue, the veil, that has in recent years been so politicized that it threatens to shape and distort the identity of young women and girls throughout the Muslim world as well as in Europe and North America.

A reveiling trend that emerged in the past two decades in a number of countries has recently gathered momentum. This trend is sustained by a socially conservative mood that spread over the Muslim world, the dissemination of faith-based literature extolling the home-making vocation of women, as well as a renewed or intensified involvement of men in matters pertaining to women's dress and deportment. I have walked into stores in Algiers where owners played CDs of speeches from self-styled religious leaders exhorting women to cover their bodies and attend to their wifely duties. I have seen prepubescent girls wearing a tightly wrapped scarf around their head atop a long skirt, holding hands with their similarly attired mothers. I do not have a daughter, but the sight of these young girls stirs feelings in me that disturb me as a woman and an intellectual. I cannot be a spectator before a trend that I strongly believe is misguided and limits women's capacity for self-determination in their bodies as part of their *human* development. I address the veil, not from its overwrought and contrived exegetic religious angle, but as an essential part of a trend that is largely *organized* and thus detrimental to women's advancement.

These young girls remind me of an experience I had when I was about seven years old while I was playing with friends outside of my home. A boy, the son of neighbors, had pulled my braids from the back while making lewd movements with his body. Alerted by my cries for help, my mother opened the door of our house and took in the scene. Since time was of the essence, she could not go back inside and put on her white veil. Instead, she pulled one of her clogs off her foot and threw it at the boy, missing him. The clog landed on my forehead, making a bloody gash. I had a half-inch scar for many years to remember the incident by. Had my mother not been thoroughly socialized in the culture of the veil, she would have simply walked the twenty feet or so that separated her from my attacker. Thirty years later, she discarded her veil. In retrospect, I wonder whether that incident had somehow worked through her unconscious mind and prepared her psychologically for the removal of her veil. The street we lived on was in a residential area, and there were few men around during working hours. My mother could have crossed it with no one noticing her. But she could not and did not. As I grew older and reflected on the incident, I wondered what would have happened had the boy been older and carried a weapon. Would the veil have prevented my mother from saving my life? Probably not, but the power of socialization on the mind cannot be easily dismissed. The veil was part and parcel of her persona; she could not be outdoors without it. She had felt utterly paralyzed before throwing her clog at the boy. Since then, many women have been able to disentangle their sense of self from the veil. But today organized efforts are made to resocialize women into the culture of the veil with the help of a whole array of frequently contradictory arguments as well as the apparent consent of some women.

To those of us who have pondered the issue, the veil inevitably makes us uneasy about its fundamental unfairness to women. The Algerian writer Kateb Yacine remembered telling his mother, who was walking him to the Turkish bath, to draw her veil over her head when she let it slip off (most likely her face and head) to breathe freely. Mother and son were on a deserted road, yet the son peremptorily ordered his mother to "put back your veil!" He wondered, years later, how he could have insisted that his mother keep her veil in place when she was out of reach of men's gaze, and whether he had not "somehow contributed to the seclusion of women."[2] He acted as her censor, oblivious to her desire for freedom in her body—a freedom that he enjoyed as a matter of fact. This thought haunted him. Yacine was one among many men who made sure that their women relatives remained in the folds of their veils.

When I was growing up, my uncle would take me, along with my aunt and my mother (both of whom were veiled from head to foot), for refreshments in the middle of the summer to a French ice-cream parlor by the shore that catered mostly to French customers. The peak moment for me was to observe my aunt and mother strenuously maneuver the tall glasses filled with cold juice and the long straw under their white veils, bending their heads over while drawing the top of their veils in such a way that they could free the right hand that secured the veil over the face according to the style that left an opening for one eye only. It was a delicate maneuver that took a few seconds, during which I expected the glass to fall and break, causing all the customers to turn around and look at us. My uncle was a highly knowledgeable man in matters of religion. He wore a red *shesh* with a black tassel that bounced in the air as he walked, and traditional pleated pants (*sarawal*) topped by a shirt, tie, and jacket à la française. He fancied himself a modernist but never said to my aunt or my mother that they could uncover their faces and enjoy their drinks, that the Quran did not enjoin a woman to conceal her face. Nor did he tell them that religion is not supposed to cause unnecessary hardship—another Quranic principle. Yet he used to lecture others about their misconceptions of their religion. His modernism was limited to taking his veiled wife and sister-in-law to an all-French spot where French women and men sipped refreshments side by side.

The normalization of the veil, its power over men's (as well as women's) minds, can be so blinding as to be deadly. In March 2002 Saudi media reported that fifteen girls died in a fire that erupted in their school in Mecca because the vice police (*mutawwa*) prevented firefighters from approaching the screaming girls on the grounds that the girls were not wearing the proper dress (a scarf over the long black *'abaya*), and contact with them would be sinful. A father was quoted as saying that "the school watchman even refused to open the gates to let the girls out."[3] Firefighters had to confront the police in order to save lives. I am not reporting this incident for its sensationalism, but to indicate that it stands at the other end of the veil culture continuum: at one end, my mother's inability to get out of the house and help me without anyone preventing her from doing so except her oversocialized self; at the other end, the special police squads enforcing the virtue of the veil at the risk of bringing death to women. In between there are as many variations of attitudes as there are styles of veiling. Such is the power of the veil that it captures the imagination, frustrates, coerces, inspires, and disempowers.

The reveiling trend coincides with an approach espoused by academic feminists that seeks to correct the notion that the veil is a sign of "oppression" but in reality makes oppression more intellectually acceptable. Although acknowledging that veiling may reinforce gender inequality, this approach uncritically and apologetically foregrounds lower-middle-class women's stated reasons for taking up veiling. Its proponents engage in various degrees of sophisticated theoretical hair-splitting in order to excavate the operative agency assumed to be lurking behind the veil, subverting its use, and turning it into a tool of empowerment. The implication is that the "oppressed" are not so oppressed after all; they have power. Faced with this newly discovered power frontier, the researcher does no more than study its manifestations.[4] She finds power in a woman's decision to veil herself, and the veil is hailed as securing a woman's ability to work outside her home, or protecting her husband from experiencing jealousy. In bending over backward to "give women a voice," adherents to this approach find it necessary to dismiss the reality of the women who object to veiling. These are routinely disposed of as being "elite," "upper class," and "Westernized." Implicitly, apologists for veiling seek to disempower local women who have a different understanding of veiling from theirs and to delegitimize these women's views while at the same time validating their own as those of dispassionate outsiders, intent upon discovering the truth of veiling or reveiling against the "Westernized" native. In this way, the outside expert shifts the charge of bias onto the "elite" native woman-qua-"Westernized." One woman elevates herself as a social-class avenger and decipherer of the hieroglyphics of the subject behind the veil; the other is banished from the realm of personhood altogether as she is deemed to only mimic the "Western" woman. It is tempting to interpret this approach as a form of intellectual masochism on the part of the researcher who dismisses the native woman as "Westernized" because she wishes nothing more than to not have to contend with the veil thing, just as the researcher does not. It represents, in fact, a new form of prejudice.[5]

My intent is not to defend the upper classes of the Middle East. Rather, I wish to draw attention to the continued and problematic academic investment in an area of Muslim women's lives in either a prejudicial or an apologetic mode. The hidden premise of the apologetic approach is that the veil is unquestionable because its wearers purportedly assume it to be so, and as long as they "choose" it, our task as researchers is to reveal its benefits for *them*. The veil, once again, emerges as a field of struggle, not only between men and women, as it has been historically, but also between native women (opposed to it) and women from non-Muslim cultures, or those hailing from Muslim cultures who support veiling in one way or another. Furthermore, the academic sanctioning of the veil turns it into a fixture of the Muslim landscape instead of an evolving phenomenon.[6]

From my perspective, veiling is not reducible to its rationalizations, be they theoretical, social-psychological, economic, or political. By the same token, veiling is not about the "right" of a woman to wear or not wear one kind of veil or another. Rights are political matters, as has been shown in the headscarf controversy that has engulfed France since 1989 and, more recently, Turkey. In France, the state passed a law (referred to as *laïcité*) on March 17, 2004, denying young French Muslim women the right to attend public schools if they wear headscarves. In Turkey, the state availed itself of the French law of *laïcité* to reinforce a long-standing prohibition against veiling in public educational institutions and compel faculty members to report and expel from their classes female students wearing headscarves.[7] The Erdogan government's attempt to remove the ban on headscarves in the spring of 2008 threw Turkey into turmoil similar to France's. The attempt was overturned by the Turkish high court as unconstitutional.[8] These controversies are part of the background of many women's decision to take up the veil. However, it is noteworthy that in both countries the veil has been made to represent something other than itself: proselytism as well as the incursion of religion—deemed backward—in politics, and thus an affront to secularism. French opponents of the scarf equated it with "sexual apartheid,"[9] and the former president of France, Jacques Chirac, called it flatly an act of "aggression" against French values.[10] In both instances, the decision that a woman makes to dress the way she pleases for whatever reason is denied. The politicization of the veil—its forced removal or its legal enforcement (as in Iran and Saudi Arabia)—hampers women's capacity to make a decision freely, just as it also compels them to abide by an intrusive law at the expense of their own conscience and judgment. More important, it contributes to confounding the veil question by defining it *unambiguously* as religious, even when the religious texts lack clarity and determinacy in the matter. In this sense, the intrusion of the state in women's lives in support for or against the veil stacks the deck against women and makes them vulnerable to giving undue credence to arguments provided by one side or the other.

I do not approach veiling from the perspective of the struggle between "tradition" and "modernity," which purportedly women resolve by opting for the veil, as a number of studies have claimed.[11] New styles of veiling are less confining to a woman's ability to move about than the old ones, and a number of veiled women throughout the Muslim world have been carrying out their professional activities side by side with men in their workplaces. Nor do I consider wearing a veil at work as ushering in a new form of "modernity." Furthermore, I do not intend to characterize veiling as representing women's "alienation," "enslavement," or "subjugation" to cultural norms. Such characterizations are unhelpful as they can easily be applied to our postmodern condition, marked as it is by a retreat from a meaningfully shared human experience and the flaunting of privatized forms of consciousness, which result in conceptions of women that are as detrimental to women's integrity as the veil might be. I instead approach veiling from an existential-philosophical standpoint that peels away the justifications that women who wear it or intend to wear it usually invoke. This is a delicate endeavor as the risk is great that a woman's rationale for wearing a veil might be discounted as a form of false consciousness, and her agency dismissed as illusory. As a social scientist, I cannot deny women's agency or substitute mine for theirs on grounds that I am more equipped to make sense of their motivations than they are. By the same token, mystifying rationalizations are not necessarily expressions of false consciousness or "agency." However, agency is not a free-floating capacity independent of the social framework within which it expresses itself; neither is it above questioning. At the same time, veiling involves *me* as a woman who grew up with relatives, neighbors, and friends who wore, or still wear, a veil. Veiling is existentially familiar to me; it has been part of my life even though I do not and will not wear a veil. Because in the popular imagination, in the Muslim world as well as in the "West," veiling has come to represent the essence of Islam, little space has been made in which this practice could be examined outside the framework of religion, or for its potentially deleterious psychological effects.

There has been a change in women's perceptions of the veil in the Middle East and North Africa. The generation of women that came of age in the 1950s and 1960s when a number of countries recovered their political sovereignty seldom took up the veil in urban centers. Coinciding with the emergence of the Islamist movement, the 1970s and 1980s witnessed a trend toward the use of veiling. Women explained their turn to the veil as the result of a heightened consciousness of the place and meaning of religion in their lives; a way of showing modesty in their dress; a protection against sexual harassment or undesirable looks from men; and a political statement, especially among women relatives of men who joined the Islamist movement. In the aftermath of September 11, 2001, the veil acquired a new meaning in Western countries as a demand for acceptance by non-Muslims and, by the same token, a manner of fighting prejudice by flaunting difference. In the context of the headscarf controversies in France, the veil has also been hailed as a tool of "liberation" for women—from imposed "assimilation" into the majority culture and, for some, from their parents' strict control of their movements. The most difficult argument to unravel is that of faith and conviction. I respect the woman who, after studying religious texts, concludes that it is incumbent upon her to veil herself, or that without a veil she would be living in a state of sin. I would, however, doubt her commitment to the veil if she has simply followed the opinion of others—men or sometimes women of religion—about the religious meaning of the veil. Faith is a personal matter even if religious practices involve the community of believers. Nevertheless, considering that the woman question in Middle Eastern cultures has traditionally been a thorny one, it is crucial that any woman who decides to wear any type of veil examine her conscience and determine whether the veil is the *only* manner for her to fulfill her spiritual needs. Because of both its role in the history of women's exclusion from social life outside the home and its resilience, the veil is overlaid with meanings that cannot be simply brushed away because a woman says so. Whenever a woman wears a veil, her act involves other women, including the girl child.

Veiling is both a discourse—a manner of thinking and talking about it, perceiving it as well as taking it for granted—and a practice. As a discourse it lies at the interface of political ideology, culture, and agency. As a practice, veiling cannot be detached from history. And it is as history—the history of women in relation to men—that it is lived and experienced by women in various parts of the world. Conflating discourse and practice "naturalizes" veiling by making it appear normative and immutable. The veil as history informs the veil as discourse, sheds light on its modalities, and helps to make out its future evolution.

The open letters that follow are offered as an invitation for greater reflection on the reasons for which women are reclaiming the veil as a constitutive part of their identity, defending it, and describing it as a means of "liberation." Over the past fifteen years, I have spoken with and interviewed numerous women, old and young, in the Middle East, North Africa, France, and the United States who have worn one type of veil or another; women who took off their veil for a while but felt they had to put it back on; and women who have been thinking of wearing one. I take these women's arguments seriously but wish to subject them to scrutiny as I am convinced that only rational reflection can advance women's understanding of themselves, particularly in times of political turmoil. For what is at stake is how women think of themselves when they are discussing religious matters, implementing what they might think is God's will, substituting religious norms for political action, or (more important) retreating into custom as a means of political protest. I explore the various angles of women's reasons and justifications for veiling, question them, and draw all the necessary conclusions, including those that might be disturbing, be unsettling, or go against the grain.

Given the history of misunderstanding of Islam as a religion and culture, there is no language in which to speak about the veil meaningfully without conveying to the reader that one is either denigrating or apologizing for a very rich culture with its inspiring ideals as well as less elevating customs. Hence I use terms that need clarifying. The expression "Muslim women," for example, does not mean that all women living in countries where Islam is the main religion are necessarily devout or in agreement with the veiling custom. Rather, it refers to the women who have taken up the veil as a way for them to display their religious affiliation. The best but cumbersome way to refer to these women would be "women-who-wear the veil-because-they think-it is-a religious-obligation-in Islam." There is no generic "Muslim woman," just as there is no generic "Christian woman"—only concrete women engaged in concrete actions. To avoid the label "Muslim men," I use the expression "male advocates of veiling." These can be theologians or self-styled promoters of a conservative interpretation of Islam. I also identify opposition movements that have used religion as a platform of social mobilization as Islamists or neofundamentalists, although these are imperfect labels.

The vocabulary of the veil lends itself to some confusion. The English concept of "veil" is rendered in Arabic by a number of terms that have different meanings in different countries and regions within countries. Besides, Quranic words referring to women's proper attire have been interpreted and translated in various ways that add to the instability of meaning. Nevertheless, at present, four words are commonly used to refer to major styles of veiling: *hijab, jilbab, niqab,* and *khimar.* The *hijab* has emerged as the standardized form of veiling across the Muslim world, coexisting with local styles.[12] It comprises a headscarf wrapped in more or less intricate ways covering the neck but not the face, atop a long skirt, long baggy pants, or a combination of both. Often the hijab is reduced to a headscarf draped around head and neck, worn over any modern style of dress. The *jilbab* consists of a long garment covering the body, a headscarf, thick socks worn with flat shoes (usually sandals), and gloves.[13] Frequently, a black face cover (*niqab*)[14] is added to the jilbab, primarily by women affiliated with a specific Islamist movement such as the Salafi (or adherents to a conservative interpretation of Islam). *Khimar* today refers to a specific way of executing a head cover that usually hugs the head tightly and cascades over neck and shoulders in a capelike fashion.[15]

To avoid linguistic confusion, I will use the concept "veil" (or veiling) to mean hijab, the most common style of veiling, and will use the two concepts interchangeably unless otherwise indicated.

In the following letters, I have changed the names of the women I interviewed, to protect their identity. Each of the first four letters considers one of the main arguments made by women and advocates of veiling or reveiling. The fifth letter discusses the reasons why women should not wear the veil.

LETTER ONE
Modesty

WHEN I WAS A CHILD, growing up in a colony, one day my maternal grandmother noticed two small swellings on my chest that slightly raised my blue silk dress. Concluding that I was becoming a woman, she said that it was time for me to wear the veil, the white piece of cotton or silk that women wore then in Algeria. My grandmother's argument struck me at the time for its bluntness. "A woman should hide her ugliness or her beauty. That's the way it should be. You must protect yourself!" she said, to my dismay.

Veiling: A Bridge over Generations

Forty years later, in 2003, Assia, a lower-middle-class, pretty young woman of twenty-two from a coastal city in western Algeria took up the hijab under pressure from colleagues and neighbors to "protect" herself. Assia aspired to a career as a singer but had worked as a clerk in a government office before she quit because of sexual harassment.

To comply with the requirement of protection, or *sutra*[1] (which in Arabic also means concealment), Assia, who had never worn a veil before, decided to follow a style of veiling (*qashabiya*) adapted from Moroccan women, composed of a long, coatlike dress—in fact a variant of a man's traditional *jallaba*[2]—topped by a hood, but she let the hood hang over her shoulders and back.[3] In this way Assia covered her body, concealing her full breasts (which nevertheless could still be made out), but leaving her hairless head and face bare. She had shaved her head because she did not like her curly hair, but I suspect that she wished to preserve her individuality, which had been erased by her long, wide veil.[4]

I thought of what my grandmother had said to me years ago and wondered what she would say today about Assia's veil. Assia was "covered" in the sense that no one could tell what she wore under her long coat or see the shape of her legs, but everyone could see her face and hair, or what was left of it. And this was acceptable to her neighbors, the vendors at the market, and the man on the street because she had complied with the new norm enjoining women to conceal their bodies.

Assia is the daughter of Mina, sixty-eight, who now lives in the south of France. I interviewed Mina on a trip to France in the summer of 2007. Mina vividly remembers the day she had to begin wearing the local Algerian white veil, a square of cloth that is wrapped around the body, fastened at the waist to a belt, and pulled over the face so as to leave an opening for one eye. Algiers women refer to it derisively in colloquial Arabic as *Bou 'Aouina*, or the "Single-Eye."[5] Mina was thirteen years old when her mother told her that it was time for her to be veiled, now that she was menstruating and her breasts were budding. Her brother, only three years older, had also remonstrated with their father that his sister was "looking like a woman" and should therefore be veiled as well as quit school. She remembers that her first veil was a bedsheet, which she had found upsetting: "Imagine! A bedsheet!" She could still recall feeling disoriented on the street when she took her first steps under her veil, which her mother had helped her to adjust. As she put it, "I did not feel good at all wearing the veil. I felt camouflaged. But then I thought this is life, you know?" She also felt "jealous" of the few girls who, because they lived in French neighborhoods in which they were less conspicuous, could afford not to wear the veil. Mina had been a beautiful young woman who worried about losing her looks under her veil. To allay her fear, she decided to make herself look good in her veil, to distinguish herself from the other veiled women. She bought expensive silk veils imported from Tunisia, which she wore over stiletto heels, and draped the silk over her face so as to make the opening for the eye larger. Her high heels guaranteed that her ankles would be exposed.

I was moved by Mina's early memories of her veiling. She had experienced the veil as a turning point in her life, signaling not only confinement but loss of femininity: the world had closed in on her. Her mother loomed large in her description of the crucial day when she first wore the veil. The poignant strategies she used to retain her individuality and femininity speak to her resentment of veiling. She had been a vivacious girl, well liked by her friends, happy to run errands for her mother and play outdoors. She was also very tough, beating back boys who tried to tease girls in her neighborhood. The veil put an end to her life of youthful insouciance that knew no gender limitation. Had she been born outside the culture of the veil, she would have continued to enjoy going outside her home and lived out her adolescence and young adulthood at her own pace. She would have had no abrupt separation in her life; she would have continued to enjoy the freedom of running, feeling the wind through her hair, and just being alive like her brother. Instead, with the onset of her menses, the biological clock ticked for her at age thirteen, and the veil fell like a curtain on her childhood. Mina's wistful description of her interrupted childhood brought back to mind the countless prepubescent girls I have observed over the years in small towns or poor neighborhoods in large cities. They would be lively, joyful, but as soon as they reached an age when they were made to wear a hijab, they would lose the spark in their eyes and become more self-conscious and less spontaneous. I suspect that the veil makes them at once more aware of their changing body and of the social limitations that such change entails for them as girls.

It was not until age twenty-two that Mina married. She spent her adolescence at home learning how to become a good housewife and fighting with her mother. On occasion when she traveled outside her city, she would take off her veil, being confident that no one would recognize her, and resume wearing it when it was time for her to return home. We seldom ask ourselves how the generations of women who wore veils felt about them. We cannot imagine them without their veils, as if they had been born with them; we expect them to wear them because *they* expected to wear them. Yet they experienced a more limited existence because of their veils.

Mina never thought that Assia, born after the independence of Algeria from France, would wear a veil. Assia's brothers had not pressured her to take it up. Mina was aware, however, that since the 1990s the social climate in her birthplace had become more conservative and more restrictive for women. Both mother and daughter, three decades after the independence of Algeria, were now going out in a hijab. Mina, a retiree from a minor clerical job in public administration—where her daughter had also worked briefly—was able to secure a French visa, a first step toward applying for residency papers, and hoped that in good time she might be able to bring her daughter to France as well. It was not specifically the veiling trend that prompted her to leave Algeria, but a feeling that as an older woman (who looked younger than her years) and a widow, the quality of her life in a provincial city had diminished. The veil was one aspect of her changed circumstances. She had hoped that her daughter would not have to play the same masquerading games with the veil that she herself had played in her youth.

The veil in this case symbolically bridges the gap that started to appear in the 1960s and 1970s in Middle Eastern societies between the older, less educated or uneducated women and their daughters, who were getting college degrees and entering the job market. Assia had had a better education than her mother, but she was now in a similar social situation, having to worry about her dress.

Shifting Modesty

It is customarily understood that modesty is a prime reason for wearing a veil. However, neither Mina nor Assia thought of her veil as a mark of modesty, although they both used the word *sutra* (protection) to explain their veiling in a somewhat perfunctory manner and with their eyebrows raised to convey doubt. Assia blamed her attire on the "bearded ones," meaning the men who in the last decade had grown beards to display their religiosity, many of whom had also joined the Islamist movement. What was it that Assia's body was protected and concealed from? Was it the long looks that men still gave her as she passed by, or was it her capacity to handle her own body? Could it be that if Assia did not conceal her body, she would not know how to dress it, would allow it to get the better of her, and would lose control of herself?

Modesty is both a character trait and a manner of acting with others that is inconspicuous and unobtrusive. Not attracting attention to oneself, not sticking out in public, is an attribute of modest behavior, as is avoidance of ostentatious display of wealth. In and of itself, modesty is a good quality that connotes some consideration for others' feelings in dealing with them. But why is the veil a mark of modesty? Can a woman not dress modestly without wearing a long coat that flaps between her feet, picks up dirt on the ground, soaks up rain from puddles, and hinders her speed when she is in a hurry? What does it mean to be modest for a Muslim woman? How does a woman reconcile the modesty of the veil with the modesty of character? What if a woman is modest in her dress but immodest in her speech and actions? Conversely, would a woman who does not wear a veil but dresses conservatively and is modest in character be termed immodest?

This discussion is hardly necessary since a key chapter (*sura*) in the Quran referring to dress does not mention "modesty," for which the Arabic word is *istihsham*. However, various translations have consistently used the concept "modest" to render the meaning of the expression "preserve [protect or guard] your pudenda [in Arabic *furuj*]." Similarly, the Arabic words *khimar*, referring to a piece of clothing, possibly a kerchief, worn by women in the seventh century, and *jilbab*, another garment that clothes the body, have been often translated as "veil."[6] Since full details of how women dressed in the heroic period of Islam are not known with accuracy, the terms used for their clothing remain open to various interpretations, as does "modesty."

> And tell the believing women to lower their gaze and be *modest*, and to display of their adornment only that which is apparent, and to draw their *veils* over their bosoms and not to reveal their adornment save to their own husbands or fathers or husbands' fathers, or their sons or their husbands' sons, or their brothers' sons or sisters' sons, or their women or their slaves, or male attendants who lack vigor, or children who know naught of women's nakedness. And let them not stamp their feet so as to reveal what they hide of their adornment. And turn unto Allah together, O believers, in order that ye may succeed.[7] (emphasis added)

A more enlightened translation avoids the word "modesty" but introduces other uncertainties:

> Tell the believing women to lower their eyes, guard their *private parts*, and not display their *charms* except what is apparent outwardly, and cover their bosoms with their *veils* and not show their *finery* except to ...[8] (emphasis added for comparison with previous translation)

It is noteworthy that this sura does not enjoin a woman to cover her face. Furthermore, the sura recommends not displaying one's breasts and beauty (in Arabic *zina*,[9] translated as "adornment" in the first text—a concept open to multiple definitions), or drawing attention to oneself by stamping one's feet, presumably to clank anklets—an obsolete custom. This last detail disappears entirely from the second translation and is replaced by "finery," an imprecise concept. In other words, in light of this sura, what passes for modesty-as-protection is a matter of opinion and choice of words instead of a clear religious obligation. Such translation uncertainties not only reveal shifts of meaning depending on what term is chosen, but also cast doubt on the routine use of such concepts as "modesty" in justifying veiling. Hence the late French historian Jacques Berque could accurately, if boldly, translate *furuj* as "sexe," which in French refers to sexual organs, and *khimar* as "shawls," instead of veils. His translation of the first part of the sura is worth reproducing as it illustrates shifts in meanings depending on language and quality of translation: "Tell the believing women to lower their gaze and contain their *sex*; not to show their adornments except that which appears, draw their *shawls* over the *cleavages* in their clothes" (emphasis added).[10]

Berque adequately interprets *juyub*, usually translated as breasts or bosoms, as meaning cleavage—a term that makes more sense considering that it is unlikely that women in the early days of Islam walked around with bare breasts. It is more reasonable to assume that some may have worn garments that reveal cleavage. Besides pudenda, bosoms, adornment, finery, and beauty all complicate the term "modesty," which becomes an umbrella concept for justifying veiling. Interestingly, men too are exhorted in the Quran to protect their pudenda (also translated as "modesty").[11] However, this exhortation has not given rise to multiple interpretations, nor has it been used to conflate dress with moral character, as has been the case with women. If one were to elide the uncertain and time-specific dress vocabulary and tell the story that emerges from two critical suras focused on women's bodily comportment, it would read as follows: women should dress in a way that does not expose their breasts and genitals or flaunt their natural beauty, so as not to draw attention to themselves and avoid harm.

It is particularly confusing for a young Muslim girl to hear that modesty is the hallmark of being a Muslim woman, and that the only sign of modesty is not specific behavior and deeds, but the veil that a woman wears. In other words, modesty as a rationale for wearing a veil hangs on a concept that is so elastic as to be meaningless. Conceivably, a woman could dress any way she wishes as long as she does not display her breasts or wear makeup. Yet women wearing the hijab also use makeup, just as many non-Muslim women do not wear garments that show cleavage or put on makeup. A Muslim woman is not more modest than another woman for wearing a veil. Modesty is not reducible to the veil. Jamal ad-Din al-Afghani, the nineteenth-century Muslim reformer, defined modesty as an individual's restraint from evil deeds that is more effective than laws. In this sense, modesty is not a virtue that can be legislated.[12]

Anthropologists correctly point out that modesty in Middle Eastern societies refers to a whole array of ideas and practices, including modalities of covering the body partially or totally; character traits such as bashfulness, humility, diffidence, and shyness; and the system of beliefs and customs that embed gendered conceptions of sex, chastity, virginity, adultery, and the like. As a character trait, modesty implies that a person seeks to downplay her achievements or skills so as not to make others jealous or envious. Such a person would refrain from bragging about her accomplishments. She may also not seek praise or credit for her accomplishments, thereby indicating that she values what she has accomplished more than she does its social evaluation. At the heart of modesty so construed is also a certain degree of self-underestimation.[13] Clearly the veil has little to do with a woman's accomplishment. It implies that a woman should humble, belittle, and feel sorry for her body—the locus of the self. At any rate, the function of the veil is at odds with its current meaning as a sign of modesty except in the narrow sense of not flaunting one's beauty. Yet a veil is not necessarily the best or only way for a woman to refrain from flaunting her beauty.[14] Does the veil then represent only one aspect of modest behavior as understood in custom and not in the religious text, or does it sum up modesty comprehensively?

Male advocates of the veil frequently argue that women must not emulate "Western" women who have no "shame" in displaying their bodies and making themselves desirable. Clearly not all Western women bare their breasts or flaunt their sexuality. Besides, why would a New York woman's choice of dress be turned into an argument for making Assia wear a garment she is not too keen on wearing? Why isn't Assia *trusted* to choose her own dress without the presumption that she would necessarily imitate the New York woman? I will return to the role that the "West" plays in the reveiling trend in my last letter. The presumption that women who do not wear a veil are emulating Western women leaves out of the discussion men's own "modesty" in dress as well as in deeds.

Din and Dunia

A regional leader of an Islamist movement in Algeria once told me that "Westerners accept that nuns wear long black dresses and cover their heads, but they object to Muslim women wearing the veil." This comment equated women who have taken vows and live in convents outside of the mainstream of social life with women whose religion is Islam, although they may or may not be practicing Muslims. He refused to accept the notion that for the veil to become the equivalent of the Catholic nun's costume, Muslim women would have to be devoting their daily activities to the worship of God alone. This is clearly not the case. Women are engaged in endeavors that are remote from a narrowly defined worship of God. They are involved in mundane tasks such as cooking, cleaning house, taking care of their children, and going to work. They meet life's problems in different ways that are not necessarily informed by religious values, just as they may be harmed by those who think of themselves as good Muslims. That some women may carve out time for their five daily prayers is undeniable, but this does not make them people whose lives are centered on worship. And it is a challenge for Muslim women, as it is for all other women who are committed to their religion, to lead their lives in ways that do not violate their faith-based ethical principles.

There *is* a difference between *din* (religion as worship) and *dunia* (life). The distinction between the two spheres of existence is being blurred by the (re)veiling trend. Making the distinction opens one to the charge of uncritically subscribing to the "Western" political-philosophical conception that posits an analytical difference between the "private" and the "public," and a procedural boundary between the religious and the political. However, conflating din with dunia is an ideological ploy that glosses over an important historical factor: traditionally in Muslim societies, the family, the locus of women's lives, has been defined as a private domain, as distinguished from the public sphere.[15] To assume that space can be divided up into a private and a public zone but moral life cannot flies in the face of reality. The inability to acknowledge that din as worship is related to but also distinct from dunia, as the totality of mundane activities, goes to the heart of the symbolic use made of the veil. Women are increasingly treated and looked at as not only inhabiting din, even though they are squarely engaged in the business of mundane activities, dunia, but also embodying it. When modesty in dress is seen as a criterion of being a Muslim woman and the veil is its most tangible sign, a very important aspect of being a woman is denied. A woman is a living being first, before being a Muslim or having a religion.[16] The foundation of the organic life of a woman, her physical body, is also denied. Denial of a woman's physical body helps to sustain the fiction that veiling it, covering it up, causes no harm to the woman who inhabits the body. Paradoxically, denial feeds into the notion that a woman is afflicted with a condition, her body, which makes her a fundamentally flawed being. Her flaw must be concealed, and the veil is the best concealment. Oddly, the veil as concealment also stands for concealing from the woman herself the fact that she is endowed with a body in the same right as a man, and that what God or nature created cannot be defined as flawed by humans.

I understand what my grandmother was driving at when she said to me that the veil conceals a woman's ugliness as well as her beauty. From her perspective, whether a woman's body is attractive or not is less important than the fact that it is a female body, and as such there is something about it that calls for its concealment. A female body is stigmatizing in a special way: it is desired, but the desire for it must be thwarted by the veil.[17] Males' desire makes the female body socially disabling. Who wants to sport a malformed arm or a hole in lieu of a face? Similarly, veiling has the effect of making a woman feel that her body is something to be ashamed of. A second Arabic word for shame or modesty, *haya'*, is close to *hayah*, meaning "life."[18] Is a woman to be ashamed of life, the life of the body? There is a fine line between experiencing shame for some objectionable action and feeling shy or cultivating shyness in oneself as a form of modesty. It is easy to take the step from thinking that a body is in need of concealment to denying that it may have needs, such as feeling the soft breeze along its limbs or having the freedom to breathe under the sun without a special cloth constraining its natural functions.

To return to the distinction between din and dunia, stressing that the veil is the most tangible sign of being Muslim means that life for women is not possible except as implementers of religious precepts. Yet with respect to the veil, these precepts are at best ambiguous and lacking in consistency. The veil is endowed with the power to transform dunia into din, life-as-usual into life-as-sainthood; the veil becomes religion in action. This of course smacks of heresy since the veil—an object—comes dangerously close to being revered! Yet, when a poor and illiterate woman wears a veil because she believes that this is what her religion requires her to do, and thus she is acting out her faith, she is dismissed as not knowing why she is wearing it.[19] The denial of a woman's body and the requirement to conceal it makes women passive objects of din instead of its active agents. It is implied that a woman cannot live her life as any other human being does—laughing, taking a leisurely walk, singing when she wishes to, buying a pretty pair of shoes, wearing makeup, earning a living—without constantly wondering whether she is in conformity with quasi-religious principles conveyed to her mostly by others. Most

significantly, concealing the body means not only concealing its existence and needs from one's mind but also running the risk of concealing from oneself the reasons behind
the requirement to don the veil. Sexual desire rears its head
when it is most denied, and giving in to it for a woman stirs
up fear, guilt, and at times the humiliation of having one's
virginity restored—the best evidence of the power of men
(not God) over women's bodies.[20] Interestingly, a twenty-
three-year-old French woman of Moroccan descent who
underwent surgery for hymen replacement at a cost of
$2,900 pointed out that "right now, virginity is more im-
portant to me than life." Yet no Muslim man needs to be a
virgin even though he too is exhorted to be "modest."[21]

Given the vagueness of "modesty," the problem is to define what part of a woman's body is likely to arouse desire
in a man. Assia's style of veil, which left her face bare and
hands free of gloves, is in keeping with schools of Islamic
law that, after multiple debates over the above-quoted sura
as well as the study of various *hadith* (traditions) attributed
to Prophet Muhammad, concluded that it was permissible
for a woman to leave her face and hands bare.[22]

If a woman conceals her breasts and legs but leaves her
face bare, is she less desirable to a man? What if a man is
attracted to a woman's eyes or lips more than to her breasts
or legs? If one agrees that men's desire floats from one part
of a woman's body to another, there is no way a woman can
be "protected" from it. Men's desire is the root cause of veils
that cover the body and face, such as the Afghan *burqa*—
veils that obliterate a woman's physical self. She must bear
the body she was born with, just as a convict must bear the
ball and chain. Concealment of the body is thus a form
of punishment as well as an apology for having been born
female, when it is not a means of redemption.[23]

Modesty and the Girl Child

Increasingly, prepubescent girls have been made to comply with the modesty requirement in dress, and many wear a layered scarf on their head before they grow old enough to wear the long garment that goes with it. The woman who makes her prepubescent daughter wear a headscarf tightly wrapped around her neck violates the texts referring to modesty and thus does harm to her daughter. There is no religious or moral ground on which to justify the forced induction of a girl into the culture of veiling. When she wraps a scarf over her young daughter, a mother conveys to her the belief that her body is an object of shame or special concern for others. She cultivates in her daughter the denial of her body; she inculcates in her psyche and emotions her natural inferiority. And this is done at an age when the little girl is vulnerable and expects her mother to defend and protect her from harm, psychological or physical. By contrast, the mother who voices her concern when her teenage daughter gives in to the reveiling trend is exercising her duty as a parent to enlighten her daughter about the historical and symbolic significance of her act, which far surpasses its indeterminate religious meaning.[24] She may not succeed, but she will have tried.

What if the little girl asks, "What is wrong with my hair, Mommy?" And what if the answer is, "Nothing, dear, but when you grow up you will have to wear a full veil. For now you will wear this scarf for your protection."[25] I have not forgotten my grandmother's comment about my body, and it seems as though this is the only thing that I remember about my grandmother so vividly. Parents teach their children not to conceal things from them, to be truthful. Yet a mother is willing to tell her daughter that she will have to conceal her hair because she is a girl. A veil not only involves the person who wears it but has significance for others, too. How does the girl in a headscarf relate to her friends in the schoolyard who run and jump freely, when her own scalp is sweating and she is worried about her scarf getting loose or being pricked by the safety pin that holds the layered folds of the headscarf under her chin? Children are inquisitive and keen observers of their environment. What does a mother tell her seven-year-old girl who asks why other girls (including those with the same religion) are allowed to feel the joy of life, but she is compelled to wearing a constraining head wrap? Would the mother tell her daughter that a man might find her hair enticing? If so, wouldn't the mother worry about fostering in her growing child anxiety and fear of men? How would the mother make sure that her daughter will not blame herself for being female since it is *her* body that presumably causes men's desire? Would the mother tell her daughter that God willed her headscarf? If so, how would the mother know that her daughter will not be resentful of God? How could the mother silence doubt in her daughter's inquisitive mind? Extolling the virtues of modesty in dress may make a good argument, but it does not satisfy a child's curiosity.

As a child, I kept quiet out of respect for my grandmother when she admonished me to wear a veil, but I never forgot that moment. I can recall the color and style of the dress I was wearing at the time, as well as the texture of the fabric out of which my mother had cut it. I had felt so good in that dress, but my grandmother had noticed only the slight swellings on my chest, not how nice I looked. A sense of unease mixed with bewilderment seized me; I did not feel well, and I left the room in silence. I was still interested in dollhouses and collecting stamps and had not given a thought to veils and womanhood. Somehow, my grandmother's comment put a different cast on the world in which I lived, which had not seemed threatening or ominous until she spoke those words.

The point is that children, young girls, do have feelings about the veil that they may not share with their parents, and although they often do not object to wearing a veil (how could they if a loving mother tells them they have to?), they may not find it an enjoyable experience. A girl likes to feel her ponytail bounce in the air and brush her neck as she runs or plays hopscotch; she likes to experience that magical and buoyant lightness of childhood. Being socialized to wear a veil at an early age is no guarantee that a young girl will accept the veil when she is older or will not take it off as soon as the opportunity presents itself. Travelers returning from the Gulf states tell stories about women who board planes clad in veils and upon takeoff fold them away. What does this masquerade mean? Who is fooling whom? How does a mother explain to her daughter this organized deception without affecting her sense of what is right and wrong? Such instances tell us that a woman may not be convinced that wearing a veil sums up her religious duty. Such instances are a reminder that wearing a veil in an age of satellite television and easier travel between countries is a very thin protection from men in the flesh or in images. The veil constrains the body, in one way or another, in spite of efforts made to represent it otherwise. Protection, one main rationale for veiling, protects no one.

Wearing Modesty, Age, and Sex

When modesty encompasses feelings in which shades of shame and shyness merge and crystallize on the female body, its meaning is easily subverted. It becomes a measure of a woman's awareness that her body is a carrier of shame, potential or actual. Modesty loses its positive meaning and gets transformed into an ideological justification of the veil. That modesty, *sutra*, is as elastic as the language expressing it is best illustrated by the varied ways in which the hijab is worn. To conceal their legs, women have taken up pants. I have seen many a young woman wearing tight-fitting jeans that hug the contours of their rears as well as shirts that flatter their breasts. In this they look no different from their non-Muslim American or French counterparts, except that they add a headscarf, elegantly wrapped around the head and face. They also wear makeup that enhances their beauty. Strictly speaking, they have complied with the customary norm that a woman's body must be covered from head to foot. But the clothing reveals more than it conceals, except for the hair, and thus the locus of modesty is in the head-scarf. Why is hair important to hide?[26] Is it more attractive to men than breasts, legs, or buttocks? Why would the hair of a seven-year-old girl be presumably attractive to grown men? A young student once explained that "because men wear their hair short, they are attracted to women's long hair." Yet men do not shave their hair, and many men sport long beards with no fear that so much visible hair might be attractive to women. Some women have also made it a point to wear a headscarf in such a way as to leave strands of hair showing through.

The focus on a woman's hair in the Muslim practice of veiling is not different from the Judeo-Christian tradition, since abandoned, that prohibited women from worshipping or prophesying with uncovered heads. This restriction did not apply to men. Ensuing debates focused on who had "authority" over a woman's head.[27]

Women who wear makeup or do not cover their hair earn the label of *mutabarrajat*, or "women who make themselves pretty." The label is used with a negative connotation since the female body must not be "displayed" or "played up."[28] Adorning the body implicitly means finding it worthy of grooming, love, enhancement, and perhaps pride. The *mutabarrajat* contradict the notion that the body must be inconspicuous, hidden from view and suppressed. I cannot stress how deeply damaging this notion is for women, especially the older generation, who wore veils all their lives and internalized the view that the body must be repressed. When considered in the context of their busy lives taking care of large families, this notion results in women neglecting themselves. They avoid grooming themselves, let themselves go, aided by their entourage that is all too quick to remind them that they are "too old," even when they are not, to "adorn" themselves. Social contempt for the female body thus turns into women's resentment of their own bodies. Consequently, women act as if they were disembodied. This does not mean that all women refrain from grooming themselves: women have traditionally used elaborate techniques of the body, but they have carefully managed their appearance outside the home so as not to indicate that they cultivated their bodies.

In the wake of the reveiling trend, age as well as marital status still matter as inducements to wearing the veil. In Algiers I spoke to three women who had been employed all their lives, but as they entered their sixties, fifties, and forties, respectively, they each took up veiling. One prided herself on not wearing the long dress, but "only" a headscarf atop her regular clothes. The others wore the hijab. They all revealed that this was their way of accepting their age. To these women, donning the veil was a sign of modesty born out of the recognition that they were not sexually attractive because they either had not married or, in the case of the sixty-year-old, had been divorced. As the fifty-four-year-old put it, "I cannot hope to be married. So, why not wear the headscarf?" What gives these women's decision to veil themselves significance is not the acceptance of age as defined in their society; rather, it is their implicit acceptance of veiling as a device that separates the sexually desirable from the sexually dead. The meaning of modesty in this case shifts once more in a way that contradicts the raison d'être of the veil: that it conceals a woman's desirability. It is commonly understood that an "older" woman may discard her veil rather than wear it, but the text of the sura shows otherwise: "As for women past the age of child bearing, who have no hope of marriage, there is no harm if they take off their (outer) garment, but in such a way as that they do not display their charms. But if they avoid this, it would be better for them. God is all hearing and all knowing."[29]

This sura connotes that an *unmarried* woman past child-bearing age (which varies with women) may be exempted from wearing a piece of clothing or *thaub*, a word that simply means garment and is not part of these Algerian women's cultural vocabulary.[30] The women were wearing versions of the hijab, not a *thaub*. In this context, modesty is as good an argument for concealing one's body completely or partially as for not wearing a veil. Age as an issue is equally important as social class in veiling. In refuting Qasim Amin's book, *The Liberation of Women* (originally published in 1899), Al Azhar University, the seat of theological knowledge, acknowledged that poor women are not under the obligation to wear the veil or refrain from work outside the home.[31]

Some argue that poor women find it economically advantageous to wear a hijab as they save money on clothes.

This may indeed be the case for individual women. However, a poor woman still must wear some clothes under her veil, which also cost money. Furthermore, she could wear the same dress just as she purportedly wears the same hijab whenever she leaves her home. The economic explanation of the hijab conceals yet another justification of veiling.[32]

Some women writers have explained that the veil serves as a device that alleviates an unconscious fear that men feel toward women's sexuality. I am not convinced that this is the case, although fear of people different from us, be they women or ethnic groups, is not to be dismissed in accounting for prejudice. However, the veil is a complex and internally contradictory custom. It connotes not only shame and desire but also contempt. Mina, Assia's mother, recounted with anger how her twenty-six-year-old son who went to France to visit her told her one morning that he was glad that he had not been born a woman. Contempt for the female body is part of an old story with which women in other societies are familiar. What makes it more important for Muslim societies is the logical extreme to which it has been taken. Mina had left Algeria to lead a better life, but her son saw to it that she would not escape the customs she left behind. He admonished her to wear a scarf on her head and enlisted his older brother to call her to reinforce his message. Both sons expressed to their mother their concern for the salvation of her soul. Mina humored them by wearing a cowboy handkerchief on her head whenever she went out of her house, but her sons were adamant that she should wear a long headscarf that wraps around her head and neck. In the end she did not, telling her sons that the salvation of her soul was an issue between her and God. This, too, is a familiar story, as Muslim mothers are often under pressure from their sons to wear a veil. Why would a son insist that his mother wear a veil? For him, the veil is the first step toward saving a woman's soul—the ultimate argument in filling a woman with fear and dread about her future. But how could a piece of cloth save a soul? The son's statement implied that a woman's body is an impediment to her salvation unless it is concealed. The slippage from the veil as guarantor of modesty to the veil as key to salvation reveals how difficult it is for a woman to be entirely sure of which function the veil she is wearing fulfills.

Since the veil has more than one meaning, how does a woman know that modesty is the one meaning that she is conveying to others through her veil? Wearing a veil is not simply a personal act; it is a *social* convention. Consequently, it is not possible to claim that veiling is a voluntary act comparable to deciding between going out shopping or staying home. Even though veiling involves willful compliance, it always takes place in a social context and responds to social norms. Social pressure to conform obscures the stated purpose of the veil, modesty. Were modesty truly the issue, there would be different ways of expressing it. A woman could tie her hair into a ponytail or roll it into a bun, which she would cover with a black net. She could wear a "modest" skirt that does not trail on the ground. But such a woman would not be considered Muslim enough. I once led a seminar with a group of professionals in Islamabad, Pakistan. I wore a conservative gray suit with a skirt that fell below the knee. The seminar went well, and as I was about to take leave of the participants, a man gracefully said that he hoped that I would come back again for another seminar, to which a woman replied, "Indeed, but only if she changes the manner in which she dresses!" This highly educated woman had been wearing the Pakistani dress and had apparently resented my suit, possibly because it put me in a different relation to men from her own. All the men wore suits. My suit located me in a professional relationship with them; her dress accentuated her difference from both her male colleagues and me. Interestingly, this woman did not mention modesty as the reason for which she found my dress objectionable. She wanted another Muslim woman, me, to comply with what *she* had complied with. This example reveals the disjuncture that often exists between dressing according to norms of modesty and experiencing modesty. Her flaunting her dress but deriding mine was all but modest; it was inappropriate and aggressive.

Headscarves, hijabs, and such accoutrements are currently known under the generic word "cover." To cover is shorthand for wearing any type of veil. It is a deceptive term that implies that women who do not "cover" somehow go about their daily activities exposed or naked. The answer to the question "does she cover?" helps male advocates of the veil to distinguish a good from a bad woman, a Muslim from a lapsed Muslim, a devout woman from a "secular" woman. A few years ago, a teenage boy in an elite New York City high school proposed to a Muslim Club, which was compiling a list of speakers, that his older sister, an anthropologist, be invited to give a talk. The president of the club asked, "Does your sister cover?" At a loss, the boy inquired about the meaning of the term. As it turned out, the sister was not invited because she did not "cover." The teenager was also surprised that at the first meeting of the club, female students were asked to sit in a different section of the room from their male counterparts. Clearly, the male leaders of the club wished to induce in their membership a sense of differentness and specialness based on "covering." Needless to say, this term is stereotypical and creates unwarranted distinctions between women. It also paves the way for conflict between women by inducing some to feel more righteous than others. Covering and covering up are close. This ideological use of the veil covers over, and deflects attention from, a number of very serious issues that women face in their lives as well as communities. It symbolizes a will to flatten out the very real individual, family, social class, and ethnic differences between women by emphasizing one common denominator, the veil. This covering up does not necessarily bring about solidarity among women; it makes women from diverse backgrounds *interchangeable*. They are all the same, at least in their outward compliance with a custom that either obliterates their physical existence or marks them as radically different beings who must wear their gender as a mark of identification, a stigma, in the manner that the Greeks used to brand noncitizens and criminals. Singling out women for veiling undermines the modesty argument for covering in at least two ways: it emphasizes the differences between women and men in a manner that is unredeemable, and it makes women more, not less, *visible*. A man does not wear a veil and does not have to be "modest" about being a man. Furthermore, veiling obscures new divisions among women between those who possess the monopoly over the virtue of modesty qua veil and those who do not.

To reduce modesty to veiling means to sever veiling from a whole configuration of ideas, misconceived notions about the nature of women, as well as gender relations, without which veiling would not exist. It means reproducing this historical configuration whether a woman is aware of its implications or not. To be crude about it, since the text mentions bosoms and pudenda, dressing in a way that does not reveal these would satisfy any requirement of appropriate dress for women. Similarly, chastity, a term that is subsumed under modesty, reads in Arabic as *'iffa*, which also means integrity, probity, and honesty. The language in which the umbrella concept of modesty is expressed is thus varied and reaches beyond sexual matters. The Arabic concept of *sitr* (colloquially synonymous with *sutra*) means not only a window curtain but also pretext and excuse. I would like to retain this last meaning, as it conveys a characteristic of the practice of veiling that is seldom if at all mentioned.

LETTER TWO
Sexual Harassment

IF MODESTY WERE A MAIN FUNCTION OF THE VEIL, women would not be the objects of sexual harassment. Yet, it is common knowledge that sexual harassment is rife in stores, markets, in the workplace, and on crowded buses, among other places. A number of women take up veiling because they feel that this is the best way to ward off men's advances. They accept the notion that the veil "protects" women, and they think that men who are not their relatives share in this understanding of the function of veiling. Although there are men who value veiled women and treat them with deference, many do not. Discussions with women reveal a serious situation that underscores the gap between ideology and real life.

Fatima, a thirty-two-year-old woman, lives with her mother, sister, and two brothers in a middle-class neighborhood in central Algiers. She had held various part-time jobs while waiting to get married. As this prospect seemed to wane with every passing year, she decided to go back to school and get a degree in business management. She subsequently found a job at a private business, rejoicing that she could now earn enough money to buy a car. After the first six months in her new position, she took up the veil, wearing loose slacks, a shirt, and a black scarf tightly tied around her head and neck. I asked her whether she had yielded to the wave of reveiling among women that had swept her neighborhood as well as the building in which she lived in the past five years. She pointed out that there were still three women in the building who did not wear a hijab, implying that she had company if she had wanted to stem the tide. She hesitated before admitting that "it's because of work." Her boss had harassed her, and she thought that if she wore a veil he would leave her alone. But after a brief letup, harassment continued. This was particularly painful for her because she had hoped to turn her life around, and finding a job, given the economic climate, had been a great achievement. Her hopes to go it alone, "without a man," seemed compromised. She was unsure of what she should do next but was unwilling to talk about her predicament to her brothers or neighbors. She took it hard, as if this were a blemish on her.

Fatima's predicament brought back memories of childhood among veiled relatives who would warn one another about such and such merchant who had "a long eye," meaning a roving eye. Some storekeepers would politely invite a veiled customer to step into a small backroom, purportedly to leisurely examine their merchandise in more comfort than standing at the counter, holding the old-fashioned veil in place with one hand and being jostled by other customers. However, the merchants' considerate approach had less to do with being culturally sensitive and more with peeking at the woman under the veil (who might let her face show), and often groping her. If a woman with a face veil is not immune from harassment, why should Fatima, whose face was bare, be "protected" from her boss's "long eye?" Fully veiled women would also report that an occasional merchant would thrust change in their hands in such a way as to rub his fingers in the middle of their palms, an unpleasant experience for a woman. Such a bold (yet all too common) gesture from a stranger was meant to convey a man's less than honorable intentions. Hence, there are many ways in which a veiled woman can be harassed just like the woman who goes out veil-free.

Denial and Complicity

The question is, if women know about sexual harassment in spite of the veil, men who are advocates of veiling must know about it too. This situation of mutual belief in the veil as protection from sexual harassment when women as well as men *know* that it is not is perplexing. It is as if women and men are complicit in sustaining a farce at the expense of a woman's dignity and sense of autonomy. Why maintain this illusion of the veil as a shield against sexual harassment?

To be an effective shield against sexual harassment, the veil, especially in its hijab version that leaves a woman's face bare, would need to be internalized by men as a deterrent of their desire for women. Women would also have to be convinced that they have no desire for men. The dynamics of male–female relations in public spaces, especially the workplace, which brings together people of both genders to discharge functions designed for the pursuit of an organization's goals, explodes the fiction of the veil as an antidote to sexual harassment. I was sitting in the office of a manager in a state institution in Algiers in the summer of 2007 when he picked up the phone and summoned an assistant to bring him a file.

Into the room came a very pretty young woman with a two-toned white and cream-colored silk scarf elegantly hugging her head and framing the oval of her face in a series of folds that cascaded over her shoulders, ostensibly to cover over her bosom. Her full breasts could still be fathomed through the tails of the long scarf and her loose blouse. There is only so much of her physical self that a woman can hide, even with the best intentions in the world. The air became charged as expressionless glances were exchanged between employer and employee. There was a slight pause as the young woman quietly left the office, followed by the man's "long eye." He cleared his throat, lit a cigarette, and resumed his discussion. The point is not that this woman experienced sexual harassment, but that it was clear to me that her looks had an effect on the manager. I thought of Assia, who had lost her job due to sexual harassment. She had been blamed by her colleagues for being too "provocative" in spite of wearing a hijab because, she argued, she vociferously objected to unsolicited passes made at her on numerous occasions. And she lost her battle to stay employed as a result. What her example suggests is that sexual harassment in the absence of laws that prohibit it has no bounds, and to expect that the custom of the veil, even if infused with a religious meaning, makes it stop is a flight of fancy. Unlike the younger generation of women who justify the veil by pointing to its protective function, the older generation who wore the veil as a matter of fact and could not conceive of life without it knew well that it did not offer protection from sexual harassment. Some defended themselves as best they could; others gave in to it.

Often, advocates of veiling ground their view that it protects women in the following sura: "Oh Prophet, tell your wives and daughters, and the women of the faithful to draw their wraps a little over them. They will thus be recognized and no harm will come to them. God is forgiving and kind."[1]

An advocate of the veil translated harm (in Arabic, *'adan*) as "molestation" in an evident attempt to link the veil with the idea of protection against sexual assault or harassment.[2] There is no need to quibble over the meanings of this sura; I will simply note that the veil as a way of recognizing that a woman is a Muslim loses its meaning in the context of a predominantly Muslim society. In practice, harm comes from men to women no matter whether they are practicing, veiled, or not. Advocates of veiling of both genders no doubt realize that contemporary societies, like their predecessors, are hardly societies of saints. Men have to be truly convinced that the veil is a moral deterrent to their sexual desires, the equivalent of the incest taboo (which also is at times violated). Yet "adultery of the eye and the heart" cannot be stamped out by the veil.[3] There is a romantic side to the a-rational notion that a veil can deter desire—a source of sexual harassment—or harm to women, including molestation. To uphold the veil as a necessary aspect of being a Muslim woman requires a suspension of disbelief that it can be an effective protection against the ills that it is supposed to "protect" a woman from. It has to be conceived as the concretization of a moral ideal that very few men can realize. This illusion is contagious as some Western women evince a yearning for the veil as a convenient way of keeping men's long looks at bay.[4] Better still, some even argue that the veil might have the virtue of freeing a woman from having to do up her hair or dress well. These are gratuitous yearnings for a mythical social order free of preoccupation with the body. Naturally, these women could wear wigs or cover their clothes with a coat. Entertaining the notion, even if abstractly, that the veil might not be such a bad custom after all makes good conversation but falls short of understanding the social and political significance of veiling.

At the root of the conception of the veil as a deterrent to sexual harassment is a seldom recognized investment of men from various walks of life in women's relation to their body. Men scrutinize women's faces, whether a woman is veiled or not, for signs of where they stand on sexual matters. Over the years I have been struck by the degree to which men are cognizant of women's methods of grooming themselves as well as the meaning for them, as men, of a woman's act of grooming herself. I remember vividly a discussion that took place over lunch with a group of male colleagues at a state-owned organization where I was briefly employed in the early years of Algeria's independence. One of them characterized a new secretary as the type that wore "kohl." He meant that she was trying to look natural but was in effect enhancing her appearance in a way that was not to his liking. He did not see the effort that this young woman was making to not offend men like him by wearing eye makeup. Kohl is usually made by rural women by grinding antimony into a fine powder, which is then applied with a hand-hewn oak pencil. It struck me as odd that this young man, educated in Paris, would know exactly what kind of eyeliner the secretary had used unless he had been keenly aware of traditional cosmetics used by his female relatives—a domain that theoretically is not his as a man. Needless to say, the secretary had probably used an eyeliner pencil, also called kohl, made by a French cosmetic firm. But my colleague seemed pretty sure that the young woman had used the traditional kohl and nothing else; *he* could tell the difference between traditional kohl and modern eyeliners. I felt a mixture of unease and spoliation at his comment.

The secretary had been denigrated for using a traditional cosmetic (if she had in fact used it), but the world of the women (including the man's mother or grandmother) who use or make kohl had also been denigrated. I later realized that my colleague's comment was not unique to him, and that it reflected a common attitude among men. Women do not make statements about how men take loving care of their moustaches or beards, or get their bodies massaged at the *hammam* (Turkish bath); they consider a man's body his private domain. However, a man not only *knows* how a woman grooms herself but has an opinion about what cosmetic device is permissible, and whether it represents a woman's modernity or traditionalism. What a woman considers her private domain becomes his.

There is a battle of the sexes occurring on a daily basis over such trivial matters as using nail polish, wearing perfume or lipstick, or choosing the color of a dress. This battle is brought to a pitch when a woman agrees to don a veil but grooms her face all the same. She may use kohl, subtle rouge, or even lipstick. There is a fine line for a man between involving himself deeply in the privacy of a woman's relation to her body and seeking to appropriate that body in one way or another, of which sexual harassment is one. Having made himself so familiar with the minutia of how and with what a woman grooms herself, and knowing that quasi-religious texts dissect a woman's body into parts that can be made visible and others that should not, entitles a man to a woman, empowers him to take liberties with her whether she likes it or not. This outcome is the functional equivalent of the effect of sexualized advertising on conceptions of women in industrial societies. In both types of societies, women's bodies are objects of manipulation for the market, in one instance, and moralized codification, in the other. Either way, women lose control over themselves by being made imaginatively (in images and texts) *available* to men.

A woman's desire to groom herself is perceived by men as playing up to them. A woman cannot groom herself for the pleasure of it, to experience a feeling of satisfaction before her reflection in a mirror, to be proud of her appearance. Everything a woman does for her body is perceived as a sign of sexual desire working through her and working her through and through. Her body is perceived as existing *for* men. In Western societies, rape is often seen as being provoked by the manner in which a woman dresses. Similar thinking underlies the notion that veiling is protection against sexual harassment.

The fiction that the veil is an antidote to sexual harassment is crucial to understanding the psychology of veiling. There is a myriad of ways in which the veil works on a man's psyche (as well as a woman's). I have referred to young Kateb Yacine keeping watch over his mother to make sure that she did not slip out of her veil on a deserted road. Yacine's recollection and delayed sorrow is instructive. A man gets accustomed to a veil (just like my mother had done) *without* thinking about its impact on a woman. He sees the veil as part and parcel of being a woman. He does not ask himself if a woman is happy wearing it, if it restricts her movements, or if it affects her conception of herself and others. The veil becomes natural, as natural as the sun, the sky, or the air that Yacine prevented his mother from taking in directly. Yacine, like other men, thought of the veil as a *normal* thing for a woman to wear, and for a man to make sure that she does. The veil appears unquestionable, taken for granted, and the reason for it self-evident. The veil exists because it must be worn. It must be worn because there are women. Women are made to wear veils. This process of *naturalizing* the veil, of making it second nature to women, conceals its ultimate justification from its advocates as well as from its wearers. The veil becomes part of the physical environment in which one lives, a familiar object on one's personal and social horizon. The reality of the person under it recedes before the symbolic meaning of the veil. By its familiarity, its taken-for-granted character, the veil represents (unfairly, if not stereotypically) the milieu in which it is worn. Veils connote a given culture, a bit like Moorish architecture represents a non-Western culture. For a man, a veil is an integral component of his identity even though he does not wear it. I always wondered why a man who may not insist that his wife wear a veil does not encourage his mother or sister to discard theirs. Men tolerate the veil even when they do not accept it. For a woman growing up in a veil culture, the process is similar, but there is a difference. She experiences the veil intimately because she wears it; it may become an integral part of her persona, but she also finds it to be a nuisance and often regrets *having* to wear it.

To return to Yacine's contrite recollection, his reaction to his mother's opening up her veil was instinctive, reflexive. He did not think much at the time about whether his mother had violated a religious or more mundane convention. The veil was no longer in place over her face; she needed to put it back on. Yacine's response was not to protect his mother from anyone since the two of them were alone on a deserted street. The reasons behind wearing the veil were not the issue for him at that moment. He was instinctively protecting himself, his identity as a male. He had been raised thinking of and seeing the veil as a marker of his identity. A person who does not have to wear a veil is a man. The reflexive reaction to veiling reveals the perfunctory character of the social functions attributed to the veil.

Yacine did not have sexual harassment, or harm, in mind. He was caught up as a growing boy in a complex identity emotion in which the veil was the most visible trigger.

Sexual harassment continues unabated, with or without the veil. The sexual core of identity is what keeps the veil alive as a custom endowed with multiple meanings, a sign symbolizing many functions. Masculinity, regardless of cultural or geographic context, is predicated upon notions of femininity. It is the degree of psychological distance that men establish between themselves and women that determines how they will define themselves and what attitudes they will adopt with women. I am reminded of a saying in the popular culture in western Algeria attributed to a mythical male: "Every man beats me, but I can beat my sister Kheira." In other words, a man's identity, even if it does not measure up to expectations, is unquestionable because it is set up against that of a woman. The veil then appears as the crystallization of the difference between being a man and being a woman *in addition* to biology. However, because the veil has traditionally been part of a cultural landscape that also shapes one's perception of the world, it is often onerous to the self to let go of it. But the shedding of their veils by a number of older women also testifies to their ability to claim an identity separate from that of their male relatives. More important, such women manage to split their assumed identity as beings-naturally-in-veils from the one they claim for themselves, namely, beings as free as men to walk under the sun with hair, ears, necks, and hands free just like any other person, anywhere in the world. These women seize their place in the human universe. Theirs is an act of self-initiated liberation from uncontrolled mystifications of religious texts. And if modernity has ever been an issue in matters of veiling, these women's act is the most courageous and resounding call for a woman's autonomy over her body. As mothers they gave freely to their societies; as women they understood, in spite of all the moralizing entreaties about their proper place in their communities, that the only way to achieve their full humanity is to claim it. And they claimed it as contestants of the right to *be* in the world. That an older woman is able to break out of the veil after having worn it for over thirty years is testimonial not only to the irrepressibility of the will to freedom but also to the fragility of the ideology that sustains veiling. These women do more good to their religion than any male advocate of veiling who strains beyond credulity to translate and retranslate words to fit his problematic conceptions of women.

Where does this leave the protective function of the veil? When a man says that the veil prevents sexual harassment, he implies two things: first, the veil protects *his* sexual identity by signaling to other men that his wife, sister, or sometimes daughter is off limits to them; second, although there is no guarantee that a woman will not be harassed, at least a maximal step has been taken. In this sense, the veil becomes a formal and culturally sanctioned step to take, sometimes reflexively, to ward off a possible besmirching of a man's own identity. This formalism works only if its male advocates conceal from themselves the fact that sexual harassment escapes their control. Desire can pierce through the veil, as it can lurk unacknowledged in the man who advocates the veil. There is a sort of virtual gentlemen's agreement that women will not be harassed if they wear the veil, and that the veil is a man's *formal* duty to himself and to other men to protect themselves from one another's desire for women. It is similar to taking an aspirin every night to protect against a heart attack. It's a step that one takes so that when a heart attack occurs, one can always say, "I did all the right things."

This conscious as well as unconscious game of hide-and-seek has become evident now that economic conditions increasingly push women to work outside their homes. The workplace cannot be gender-segregated, and women often hold positions of responsibility that place them as supervisors of male colleagues. Some of these women wear the veil even though they are in positions of power over men, which theoretically precludes their fear of harassment. However, many do so not because they worry about harassment but because they are eager to gain what they believe is acceptance from their subordinates. Paradoxically, for these women the veil acts as a device to erase the superiority of their position over men while at the same time enhancing men's identity as men, as I will discuss in another letter. The veil in these instances reduces a woman's professional achievement to something for which she must apologize. "I am only a woman," she seems to be saying. "I agree with you. But I am a decent woman who wears the veil, and as such I hope you will help me to carry out my functions." The veil is thus relegitimized, and any status incongruity that a male working in a service directed by a woman might experience vanishes because his identity as a man is formally preserved. The woman has done a womanly thing by wearing the veil. She has satisfied his sense of identity wholeness.

I frequently wonder why it is necessary to engage in these games and invest a great deal of energy in them that could be directed to more useful endeavors. Why cannot a man just accept that a woman need not be veiled, just like he is not? And if a woman's veil is a symbol of modesty that protects her from sexual harassment, why do men not show modesty in their behavior toward women by refraining from harassing them?

LETTER THREE
Cultural Identity

AMINA, a senior in a New York City college, wore the hijab, a long and dark-colored flowing robe and a layered scarf wrapped around her head and draped over her shoulders, for a year in 2003. As a second-generation immigrant from Southeast Asia, she was critical of the treatment of Muslims in the media. She felt that wearing the hijab would show that she is proud of her Muslim heritage while at the same time asserting her right to be different and to be respected in her differentness. A year later, she took her long garment off, keeping only her headscarf on, which she now wrapped around her head so as to leave her ears free. She told me that when she wore the complete hijab, she did not experience any "emotional gain." In addition, although she had noticed that some people looked at her inquisitively in the subway, by and large she had not encountered any offensive reaction. It was as if she had anticipated some exciting struggles with strangers on her daily commutes but was disappointed that none materialized.

In the post–9/11 era, experimenting with the hijab (because for many it is an experiment) has emerged as an increasingly attractive method for women from Muslim communities in Europe and North America to display pride in their culture. A young woman wishes to tell the world that she is not afraid of diffuse hostility toward Muslims, that she is willing to confront it head on by sporting her identity. What better way to do this than by wearing a hijab—one of the most tangible, visible, and recognizable signs of difference other than skin color? There are obvious reasons for this attitude. The veil has traditionally been the object of contempt for Muslim cultures as well as a stereotypical symbol of the assumed backwardness of Islam as a religion. Conversely, in situations of political crisis, not wearing a veil is sometimes perceived as a rejection of one's cultural background. In a fictionalized account of real-life occurrences, a seventeen-year-old French Muslim woman told her mother, "This is important, Mom; it is my religion, I am a Muslim and proud of it! . . . I don't want to be like you anymore and play at being French. . . . And I am sick of all those whores!"[1] Seizing on a reviled but salient aspect of one's culture and flaunting it as a badge of honor is part of a process of reclaiming and asserting a cultural identity. However plausible this process might seem, it is not as simple as it appears.

For Qama, a nineteen-year-old woman of Middle Eastern descent, wearing the hijab is a constant source of self-examination and questioning to which the garment provides only a partial answer. Qama started wearing the headscarf (which she refers to as hijab) when she was thirteen, in the aftermath of 9/11, after her parents came under close scrutiny by the Federal Bureau of Investigation. Subsequently her father disposed of his Islamic clothes and her mother discarded her long dress, keeping only her headscarf on.

Around the same time, Qama's good friends, a couple of Middle Eastern origin, had come under similar pressure by the police to change their dress too, including, for the wife, the removal of her headscarf. These incidents were the triggers of Qama's decision to wear a headscarf atop her regular clothes, typical of those of other young New York women her age. She felt that her parents as well as her friends had too easily (albeit understandably) given up what they believed in. She was also angered by the anti-Muslim sentiment and climate that contributed to her parents' and friends' action. By taking up the hijab, she wished to "make a statement, to say that you don't have a hold on me and tell me what to do. Given the circumstances, I'm going to do what you don't like me to do. What are you going to do about it?" Interestingly, Qama does not explain her decision as a form of resistance, as many researchers have in dealing with (re)veiling. Qama's is a complex act of defining herself as a woman who lives across cultures (Middle Eastern and American), whose sociopolitical commitments place her somewhat at odds with other women who donned the hijab.[2] Deemed a woman "of color" in spite of her fair looks, she attempts to negotiate the racial and ethnic categorizations prevalent in American society without losing her cultural integrity. Wearing a headscarf allows her the insights of a participant observer of prejudice stemming from the conflation of race, skin color, politics, and religion, which the hijab evokes in people. The hijab contributed to a paradoxical sundering of her self-identity: "It is part of me; yet it is not me. Many parts of me go against it." In the end, Qama felt that the hijab "is a reactive [response]; it asserts an identity that was questioned, and I think that I was creating my identity, but in a sense, I did not create anything. I took up a challenged identity and made it my own."

The reveiling trend in Europe and North America emerged as an outgrowth of a movement that started in the Middle East in the 1980s. The rise of new fundamentalist movements among young men eager to revive and restore old practices sparked discussions as well as concern about what it means to be a Muslim, to live one's life as a Muslim man or woman. The veil appeared one more time as a marker of difference from the globalized cultures of the "West." The tussle between Muslim minorities and European states brought to the fore the veil, once again claimed as a means of asserting and protecting cultural identity. In an age of rapid communication, responses of Muslims in one country affect Muslims living in another. In the wake of the Abu Ghraib torture scandal, the spectacle of a Lyndie England walking a naked Muslim man on a leash did little to quell the hunger that young Muslims in the West have felt for acceptance and respect. The veil seems to provide a safe albeit anachronistic response.

Permutations and Vagaries of Identity

On occasion I have seen a woman clad from head to foot in a black, coatlike garment, leaving only enough space for the eyes from which to see, crossing the street in New York. I do not know whether such a woman is the wife or the fiancée of a man who insists that she wear the niqab-style veil or whether she has decided to take it up on her own. I must admit, however, that such a sight always startles me. I was similarly taken aback when, upon entering a shop in the old city of Damascus, it took me a few seconds to realize that there were two human forms in black sitting near the counter. Their faces were entirely covered in black cloth, with no opening for the eyes. I felt crushed by their anonymity and the obliteration of their being. After these forms stood up and left, the shopkeeper explained to me that the women were not Syrian but had come from Iran on a visit to some of the Shi'i shrines. The feeling I experienced bothered me for two reasons: First, I come from a veil culture and should not have been surprised. So why was I? In my defense, I had never seen this style of veiling before. Second, I wondered whether this was the feeling that veiling evokes in non-Muslim people. Upon reflection, I realized that my surprise at the two forms—because they were seated, for a few seconds I could not make out what they were exactly—was due to my reading the black shroud as an assault on my own being as a woman. A few hours earlier, I had tried to enter the mosque of Sayyida Ruqayya, a great-granddaughter of Prophet Muhammad's. I had been properly dressed for the occasion, wearing loose slacks, a wide, long-sleeved shirt, and a white scarf. I was stopped at the entrance of the mosque by a small man who advanced toward me with arms outstretched, holding a large piece of cloth, grayish from dirt and use. He intended to cover me with it. I instinctively stepped back, surprised by the man's brashness, and pointed out that I was properly dressed and would not wear such a dirty piece of cloth. He shot back: "It is cleaner than you!" This put an end to my ability to visit a mosque built in honor of a woman. The day before, I had had no problem visiting the Ummayad mosque. I could not help thinking that this man, the keeper of moral hygiene, seemed to have a very long arm that also reached into the shop where the two obliterated women had sat. This incident convinced me, if I needed convincing, that the veil is a man's affair before it becomes a woman's.

When I reflect back on this incident, I feel mortified that a complete stranger would take it upon himself to assault me verbally, exercise his power over me (after all, he did prevent me from visiting the mosque), and expect me to comply with his will. And all this was done in the name of Islam to another Muslim, me, a woman. Even the policeman whom I had the receptionist call was not able to help. I had expected him to perhaps admonish the man, even arrest him for attempted battery, or for disturbing the peace of the mosque. But he was as powerless as I. He did, however, walk me outside of the mosque and explain to me that although the mosque was in Damascus, it was controlled by the Iranian government, which claimed its spiritual ownership. He went on to tell me which other mosques I should avoid as they too were in the hands of Iranian guardians. I wondered why the stranger at Sayyida Ruqayya mosque thought that he had power over all the women who sought to enter the mosque, be they Iranian pilgrims, Syrians, or foreigners like me. The sense of helplessness I felt before this keeper of the faith was bottomless. It rankled that he would derive power from humiliating a human being; his face exuded not only contempt for me but also defiance. My misery buttressed his power and arrogance. The denial of my humanity was the foundation of his. He was powerful because I was powerless. That he could get away with his action even when the policeman came around hurt even more. Why did he not fear the police, and why did the policeman not do anything? Did the policeman feel that his uniform, his gun, and the law he represented were powerless before the sanctified chauvinism of the stranger? Could it be that the policeman agreed at some level with the guardian? At any rate I felt alone.

The receptionist had looked at me with a mixture of surprise and excitement. He had called the police at my request when he could have easily refused to do so. But he could do no more for me. The scene was surreal: a woman saying that she had been terribly wronged by a man holding his dirty veil in his hands as some sort of evidence of her wrongdoing; the receptionist watching intently everybody's moves; and the policeman with an expressionless face. All of this happened because a man decided that a woman, a fellow Muslim, was worthless. For him, I had no identity except the flimsy one he had sought to make me wear. I did not matter, with or without the police. As I walked away from this scene, I wondered why any woman should wear a veil that would help this man or anyone like him assert himself over her. The liberty that the guardian arrogated to himself to define me as "dirty" was an act of the will that spoke volumes about his fetishistic conception of the veil, as well as his contemptuous dismissal of women. He did not ask himself whether I might be a good person because he did not see me as a person. He was unconcerned by his less than modest behavior in both his act and his word. He sought to crush my resistance to his will, my rejection of his dirty cloth held up to me at arm's length as one would a screen, by brushing me aside as dirt.

This incident points to the configuration of power, politics, and gender that encloses cultural identity like a cocoon encloses a chrysalis. Sayyida Ruqayya's guardian was empowered as both a man and a guardian of a religious shrine to assert his conception of *my* identity regardless of his lack of expertise in religious matters, given that he was not a religious figure. He knew better than I how I should dress, and how (his) Islam defines me. It is of no consequence that he was a Shi'i Muslim, and thus stricter on veiling matters, or that he strayed in his upholding the gender order among visitors (in the midst of whom there were no Western tourists). He was simply empowered over me: I had only one choice, to wear his veil or get out of the reception area of the mosque.

The definition of cultural identity when grounded in quasi-religious notions thwarts a woman's will and agency. Guardians of shrines, states (Muslim or non-Muslim), and neofundamentalist movements all have a hand in it, draw circles around it, permutate its terms this way or that. During the controversy over the headscarf, the French state defined and imposed its identity in as heavy-handed a manner as the guardian of the Damascus shrine had done. It got rid of headscarves by expelling the students who wore them from public high school.[3] Women were presented with a choice that no one should have to face: remove their headscarves because the French state considers these signs of proselytism or leave school. Even more remarkable is the Turkish state's ban on headscarves in public workplaces as well as schools. When assertive students (many of whom were from rural families that migrated to the city) braved the ban, their government hounded them. Women were humiliated into taking off their headscarves before university officials in a show of force by powerful male radical secularists defending their own identity. To secularists, the headscarf represents the intrusion of religion into politics.

The ill-fated decision of February 9, 2008, by the Recep Tayyip Erdogan government to lift the veil ban meant that women would be free to decide whether to veil themselves. Yet banning the veil is as much a political act as is mandating it. Turkey (like France or Germany) is thus on a par with Saudi Arabia and Iran. Each sees the veil as standing for religious identity. Women are held hostage equally by radical secularists and Wahabists,[4] Islamists and Shi'i Muslims. None of them trusts women with the capacity to decide for themselves how to manage their bodies and whether to wear a veil. None of them has asked women for their opinion in the matter. Thus, whether she is in a shrine in Damascus or lives in Europe, a woman bears the brunt of the politics of cultural identity as crystallized in the veil.

To return to the women who voluntarily take up a hijab to make a statement, a few points need to be clarified. Feeling comfortable in one's culture and asserting its worth is one thing. However, reducing the essence of that culture to the veil is another. A woman who lives in a non-Muslim society but does not wear a veil is no less proud of her culture than the woman who wears one. She may express her pride in writing or speaking publicly about her culture. She may leave her mark as a Muslim woman by achieving fame and honor. I am not convinced that wearing a scarf on one's head or wrapping one's body in a long garment in New York or Paris helps to reduce prejudice against Muslims or elicits greater respect for them. It may, it is true, get people accustomed to the idea that there are people among them with different habits. But I suspect that they know that already. And is this reason good enough? Is the veil the best response to anti-Muslim prejudice? Is abstaining from drinking wine (a religious prohibition) at professional meetings not just as good as wearing the veil? Is abstaining from eating pork not an equally important way of asserting one's difference from others? Is the veil really about cultural difference? How about wearing a pin representing a star and crescent, or a pendant inscribed with the name of God, as some women already do, or a green band around one's arm as a sign that one is a Muslim, if one needs to display one's religious affiliation? There is no compelling reason why the essence of Islam should be reduced to a veil, and women singled out as its embodiment. The veil intrigues and beguiles; it shocks and repels. However, it also trivializes and objectifies religion.

In this context, it is important for women to know the pros and cons of the veil and demystify its meanings before making up their minds about wearing it. They can no longer leave it up to states, to male politicians, to legislate how they should dress, what constitutes "modest" dress, and whether a veil is the only way that a woman should assert her Muslim identity. In the end, a question is inescapable: Why should a state, "Western" or Middle Eastern, legislate a woman's body? I am reminded of the debates over abortion in which states, usually led by male legislators, decide whether a woman should or should not have an abortion. Yet only a woman knows intimately whether she can carry a child to term or is able to care for it when it is born. Similarly, only a woman should be able to decide whether she should wear the veil. More important, only a woman should be able to determine whether the veil sums up her commitment to her religion. Politicians, be they secularists or faith enforcers, are bent upon protecting their identity by appropriating women's. They use the veil as a cultural flag, if not a weapon against women. Yet without women's consent, complicity, or passivity, they would not be able to fight one another over the appropriateness of women's attire. The veil-obsessed governments do not legislate men's dress as they do women's. Fatma Benli, a Turkish woman who has fought discrimination against women (such as herself) who wear the headscarf, rightly pointed out that the veil controversy in her country distracts the state and society from focusing on domestic violence, honor killings, and a criminal code that is biased against women.[5] Ms. Benli's decision to wear a headscarf must be respected; I give credence to her feeling that the headscarf is part of her "personality" and her "wholeness." However, discrimination cuts both ways. A woman compelled by law to wear any form of veiling is also the object of discrimination, given that the law does not codify men's attire. Furthermore, discrimination in dress adversely affects a woman's perception of herself, as I will explain in my last letter. Women need to address this framework of extremes (mandating or banning the veil) before they opt for the veil as an appropriate act. The veil is embedded in a constellation of ideas, perceptions of women, and ideologies that give it substance and meaning.

A number of women in Muslim communities in North America and Europe are not allowed by their parents to attend high school unless they wear at least a headscarf. These women avail themselves of the language of cultural identity to explain their compliance with their parents' will. One justification is as good as another in a climate of revivalism, willed or imposed. The political uses of the veil by states have called out in women responses that are equally political. Muslim identity when reduced to the veil represents a political statement made by women in response to the excesses of fear and prejudice against Islam. But should women bow to these pressures by asserting an identity that rests on a piece of clothing? Is the reduction of Muslim culture to a garment the only way to force respect from Western nations? In thinking that it is, women in reality ask for sympathy on the grounds of religious diversity, while at the same time demanding special treatment that increases their difference from others in a way that marginalizes them. Are they not demanding that their colleagues treat them differently from other workers? In January 2008 Harvard

University rearranged the schedule of the Quadrangle Recreational Athletic Center on an experimental basis to set aside hours for women. The move was a response to a petition from Harvard's Islamic Society and the Women's Center. The point is not that Muslim women, the beneficiaries of the change, should not have a space of their own. Rather, it is the reason provided for it, namely, the protection of "modesty"—an old justification for veiling—and feeling "uncomfortable" (clearly for religious-cultural reasons) about exercising in the presence of men that is objectionable.[6] Presumably these students take courses alongside males and would not think of demanding sex-segregated classes. Furthermore, there is exercise gear that does not reveal a woman's shape. What appears to be a successful act of cultural identity assertion should not obscure its less evident meaning: it sanctions practices and customs that are usually presented as religious and that have harmed women. Harvard gave its official stamp of approval to a revivalist trend that is contested by many women throughout the Muslim world.

Identity for What?

Is it possible that the movement back to the veil signals a fundamental change in the meaning and function of veiling? After all, a number of women have taken up the hijab against their parents' will and claim that they have felt empowered by it. At first glance it seems as though women in various hijab styles, some less "modest" than others, have brought about a change in the manner of wearing them. However, no matter how tight-fitting their pants are, these women all cover their hair. In their hair they reach the limit of how much liberty they can take with a custom that finds its logic in the concealment of the body. It might be argued that perhaps, in the long run, the headscarf will lose its significance and its length. In due time, it might even be discarded altogether. The veil could just wither away as a useless custom. Forty years ago, city women in a number of Middle Eastern countries thought that they had entered the postveil era. Little did they know that their daughters' and granddaughters' generation would bring back the veil as a badge of pride. The veil remains the least elevating and most politicized custom, which does little to move women forward toward human freedom.

It will not do to argue that young advocates of veiling have no uplifting philosophy, system of ideas, or ideals to embrace in a globalized world bent upon dissolving primordial ties and erasing group solidarity and identity. I believe, on the contrary, that these are challenging times requiring inventive ways of carving out a space for meaningful action in a world rent by war, social injustice, torture, and poverty. Looking backward to the veil and seeking to rehabilitate it does not transcend the history that burdens it and without which it would not exist, namely, that biology is social destiny.

LETTER FOUR
Conviction and Piety

I WAS IN MY HOME in Algiers in 2007 when a friend, Anissa, rang the bell. I opened the door to a woman with her head tightly wrapped in a blue and white scarf, wearing a loose, long-sleeved tunic hanging below her hips over black slacks. I was surprised that Anissa had taken up the hijab as I knew that neither she nor her three daughters had ever worn it. As she entered the hallway, she immediately said, in anticipation of my question, "I am wearing it out of conviction. You can well imagine that if I did not wear it during the years when Islamists were pressuring us, I would not be wearing it now that they are no longer a threat." I was puzzled by her quick invocation of "conviction" as the reason for which, in the nine months that I had not seen her, she had donned the hijab. Anissa is a fifty-four-year-old retired professor of French; she had started to supplement her monthly pension with teaching French at a state-run career development agency.

Over coffee, I asked her how she came to be convinced that the hijab was the right thing for her to wear. She recounted that during the month of Ramadan, she had gone to the mosque every night with her husband for the additional prayer called Tarawih. When inside the mosque, she put a scarf over her head, as is customary, before removing it upon her return to her home. As she saw it, keeping the headscarf on was easier and more convenient than putting it on and taking it off. I could not help pointing out that donning the *hijab* to avoid the trouble, as it were, of putting the scarf on and taking it off was hardly a sign of conviction. In a peremptory tone she put an end to the discussion, stating that she indeed felt convinced of the necessity to wear the hijab.

A few days later, while riding a particularly crowded city bus in midday heat, I made room for a young woman in a hijab who had just gotten onboard. She was sweating profusely and her cheeks were flushed. As she took out her handkerchief to wipe off the sweat from her brow, we fell into a conversation during which she revealed that she was new to the hijab. She was on her way to a housing agency to check on her application for an apartment. She was engaged to a man who had made it a condition of their marriage that she wear the hijab. She was not too happy about it, but she loved her fiancé and was eager to please him. This conversation brought to my mind a similar discussion I had had with a leatherwork artisan in the Qasbah, a man in his fifties, whose business had fallen on hard times due to lack of supplies. He had bemoaned his only daughter's acceptance of her fiancé's stipulation that she not only wear a hijab but also quit her job. The father had been proud of his daughter's achievements: she had received a degree in business management and had found a promising job. He was outraged at the prospect of seeing his daughter become a full-time housewife. He was also particularly upset by his daughter's rationale for acquiescing to her fiancé's demands. He reproduced it word for word: "Do you really think that work is the answer? Look at you, you worked all your life, and now you have to close down your store and work as a vendor on the street!" His daughter's comment had stung him, but there was nothing he could do to convince her to resist her fiancé's will.

As I was mulling over the role of the veil in marriage, I had the opportunity to chat with an irate young female handicrafts vendor, dressed in jeans and T-shirt but wearing a headscarf artfully set askance on her head as a wickedly attractive little hat might sit on a Hollywood actress's head in a 1940s' movie. She took issue with a radio program broadcast the night before that had a female listener from France, apparently an Algerian immigrant, objecting to the veiling trend in Algeria. The vendor felt strongly that the caller, living in France, did not understand that young women like her wore the hijab out of "conviction." She acknowledged, however, that there were some who wore it for convenience, to placate a father, brother, or husband, or even, as she put it, "to go out to have fun." But *she* was different. Yet I could not help thinking that this woman was putting on an act, as if trying to convince herself that she was doing the right thing by wearing a scarf on her head.

Conviction as Strategy

These cases raise questions about the meaning of conviction. Does it mean that a woman allows a fiancé or a relative to persuade her with forceful arguments to wear the hijab? Does it mean that a woman has listened to talks by religious leaders about the veil and discovered that by not wearing one she was in violation of a religious obligation? Or does it mean that a woman has studied religious texts on her own and found sufficient and compelling grounds for taking up the hijab? That some women wear a veil out of a genuine religious conviction is undeniable. Years ago I interviewed the wife of a member of AMAL militia in her home in the Bek'aa Valley in Lebanon.[1] She forcefully argued that the veil does not represent inequality but complementarity between women and men. The veil reflects the natural differences between men and women. From her perspective, it is the religious duty of a woman to display modesty in her dress, educate her children, and take care of her husband. These tasks are no less important, she stressed, than working outside the home. The veil, in her view, is part and parcel of being a good Muslim woman; it is not an obstacle to a woman's advancement, including working outside her home. In 2004 a similar argument was offered by a female member of the Movement of Society for Peace (MSP) in the city of Blida, near Algiers, who worked in an office in a hijab.

However, although many women claim conviction as their motivation, they also use the veil for strategic reasons to pursue various goals. The elasticity of "conviction" as an argument for wearing a veil is best illustrated by Amina Wadud, an American convert and advocate of gender equality. After carefully studying the Quran text, she reached the conclusion that the hijab is not a religious obligation. Nevertheless she wears it as "part of my more public participation and do so whenever I dress for campus, for professional or public engagements, business meetings, community affairs, and interfaith forums." She removes the hijab when gardening, running errands, and after a conference "to avoid a rigid stigma."[2] This apparent masquerade is carried out in the context of lectures praising the Quran for its egalitarian message. Wadud thinks that "reinvesting new meaning into old symbols is a necessary part of Islamic progression."[3] I am at a loss to understand what new meaning could be imparted to a symbol of gender inequality. Unlike other customs, the veil cannot be infused with meanings other than those that have historically been invested in it by its advocates, wearers, and detractors alike, and without which it would cease to exist. Admittedly, a woman runs the risk of not being heard by faith-conscious men should she not wear the hijab when she discusses gender issues with them. But it is also true that there is no guaranty that she will be heard when she wears one. She may be *listened* to politely, or opposed less politely.

In a moment of candor, Wadud linked the slavery past, when a woman had no say in her nude or dressed body, to the Muslim present, when she can choose to cover her body "to control their [men's] lust."[4] Choice in this context is not between alternatives, one better than the other or at least equal in value. Rather, it is a choice of strategy the design of which is flawed. The strategy of donning the hijab to bring about change (that would include making the hijab redundant) means that a woman is still ambivalent, unsure that the hijab is not really a religious obligation. No male advocate of the veil is fooled by a woman who, wearing a cover on her head, argues for equality based on religious texts. The illusory nature of the strategic use of the veil by women advocates of change is best exemplified by the currently unhindered revival of veiling in Muslim as well as Western societies. The veil has no intrinsic human emancipatory value.

By comparison, Anissa's claim that she took up the hijab out of conviction appears less disingenuous and more ritualistic in character than the deliberate and calculated decision made by Wadud, the more knowledgeable gender-equality advocate. Anissa made no pretense to bring about change. However, her use of conviction is a misnomer, an excuse she put forth to hide her embarrassment at wearing a dress (in front of an old friend of hers) that she was not thoroughly convinced she should be wearing. A number of considerations need to be taken into account to understand Anissa's strategic use of "conviction" as an alibi for her use of the hijab. Anissa's husband had shown increased signs of religiosity in the past few years, even though he had always been observant of his prayer duties. In various conversations with me, he had frequently expressed worry about raising three daughters in a city such as Algiers in which safety had decreased. Two of the daughters, in their late teens, had started performing their prayer rituals daily when they came home from school, slipping into black dresses to accomplish the ritual, as a sort of veil initiation. Anissa had been teaching a group of adults, among whom were a few females in hijab. Despite her high-paying position, she had perceived the presence of these women as diminishing her own status in the eyes of the male students. From Anissa's perspective, wearing a hijab killed two birds with one scarf: she preemptively allayed her husband's diffuse anxiety, and she gained additional status among her adult students. The all-female family that her husband headed was safe and secure behind the mother's scarf and the daughters' prayers. It was in harmony with the reveiling trend that swept their city. In the wake of Anissa's unconvincing display of conviction, friends were quietly yet pointedly told that the girls had started praying, as if this were an extraordinary event.

It is important to note that Anissa was not coerced by any man, least of all her husband. She sized up her situation and that of her family and deliberately took up the veil. In this sense, she felt that this was a pragmatic course of action to take. She could have just as well continued to live her life as before, devoting the month of Ramadan to intense prayer and spirituality, and continuing to teach without wearing a tightly wrapped scarf around her head. She was under no threat and in no danger from anyone. She chose instead a path in which she also involved her daughters. It is precisely this kind of attitude that needs to be understood and addressed. Anissa would not admit that she was perhaps overreacting, that it would have been more important for her daughters and their potential daughters to buck the veil tide. In fact, she had found an additional and vain reason for wearing a hijab: she started wearing pants, which she had never worn before, and felt good in them.

Anissa acted preventively, second-guessed her husband, and answered what she felt was his secret wish to see her wear a hijab. This was no doubt a move that pleased him, although he asserted that he had initially opposed it. In this conjugal psychological game, Anissa found some comfort in defining herself as a virtuous wife and mother of three daughters. Hers was a symbolic gesture that she expected to compensate for her daughters' going out without veils. Yet no one in her entourage had voiced any criticism of the daughters. Besides, the neighborhood where she lived was a middle-class one in which as many women wore a veil as did not wear one.

In this context, Anissa was not entirely wrong when she told me that this was her decision and that she took it out of conviction. Yet a religious conviction might be expected to follow an examination of religious texts, a discussion of the role of the veil in religious dogma and ritual, the otherworldly consequences of not wearing it, and so forth. This is not what happened in Anissa's case. Her decision to don the hijab was the result of considerations that were more social than religious. It won't do to say, "But this is exactly what the problem with Islam is. It is a religion and a way of life." However, Anissa's decision to wear the hijab was divorced from any concern for religious duty. It was more in keeping with a rational choice based on a maximization of potential gain and minimization of loss; it had not stemmed from concern for salvation, spirituality, or the achievement of a moral-ethical goal—although these could always be tagged on as additional reasons for taking up the hijab. It reduced religion to a formal act of pleasing others who had not made explicit demands on her. Her case points to the manner in which individual women manage social pressure. Because she is the one who took the decision, it appeared to her as free and unconstrained.[5]

Conviction and Piety

The full extent of Anissa's turn to the veil raises the issue of women's agency. If a woman like Anissa invokes "conviction" but uses this term to mean that she convinced herself that she should follow the veiling trend, she exercised her agency to conform to an outward trend, not an inner certitude. Thus, social conformity trumps religious duty, and the external side of conviction is substituted for its internal, substantive side. It is true that over the years Anissa had not neglected her prayer duties, and that she perceived herself as a "believer." Therefore, taking up the hijab may have been an expression of piety rather than conviction. However, a woman may be pious without wearing a veil. What is the relationship between conviction and piety? The *American*

Heritage Dictionary defines piety in two ways, as a "religious devotion or reverence to God," and "a position held conventionally or hypocritically." I do not intend to impugn Anissa's integrity and accuse her of bad faith. Nevertheless, her use of "conviction" to mean conformity concerning a practice, veiling, that is usually upheld by women and men as a marker of gender reflects an understanding of piety as a matter of conventionality, if not convenience.

How can one tell the difference between a woman who wears a hijab out of conviction and one who does so for conventional reasons? There is no way of telling. Besides, a woman may or may not reveal the complexity of emotions, thoughts, and beliefs that lie at the core of veiling. This is why it is important that a woman knows in her heart of hearts why she has decided to take up a veil. Considering that the reasons for wearing a hijab vary with different women in different circumstances, conviction and piety cannot be said to be the main ones. This only means that there is a slippery slope of motivations and casuistries that surround veiling; veiling lends itself to justifications on religious as well as purely conventional grounds. In this context, agency must be distinguished from consciousness—the capacity to see through the myriad contingencies that determine the "choice" that a woman makes for the good. And the good is universal.

Piety is a personal engagement with religion, as exemplified not only in matters of worship but also in the conduct of one's daily life. What if an organized movement seeks to foster its version of "piety" in women by presenting the veil as an obligation, a sign of acceptance of God? And what if that group upholds one method of being pious and presents it as normative? The group could be led by a woman who would speak to other women as one of them and would thus find a receptive audience. This has been the case of the Egyptian Heba Rauf Ezzat, an articulate advocate of women's rights within the framework of Islamic law, who sports and defends her headdress.[6] Furthermore, the piety or "mosque" movement that has emerged in many Middle East countries, including Egypt, Jordan, and Syria, is hailed as a sign of women staking a place for themselves in discussions of religious matters specifically addressing women's issues as well as their spiritual needs. On the one hand, it is a step in the right direction that women come together and express their thoughts and feelings. However, such discussions are led by women who are often dependent on male theologians' interpretations of texts (not all of whom are amenable to the promotion of women's interests and needs), use the same methods, and arrive at similar conclusions.[7] Besides, this movement aims at informing women about their religious duties and responsibilities as good Muslim wives, mothers, and daughters, not enlightening them about the sociopolitical implications of looking inward and investing their energy in examining each and every gesture they make in their daily lives for its religious authenticity or relevance. In times of political turmoil and economic hardship, movements that urge women to focus on the minutia of their everyday lives also result in taking women's attention away from participatory engagement in the lives of their countries and help to reconcile the poor and vulnerable among them to their social condition. In this sense, the mosque movement contributes to the integration of women in the larger intraregional trend that seeks to further blur the line between the sacred and the profane, din and dunia. It is a force of social conservatism regardless of its occasional benefits for individual women. In this, the movement is hardly unique; it is part of a long tradition in Egypt, for example, of faith-based organizations such as the Muslim Brotherhood creating a feminine wing for agitating among women.[8] It goes without saying that the involvement of women in religious movements is not specific to Middle Eastern societies: it has its counterpart in Western societies among evangelists.

Rural women most in need of change in their lives are most affected by these movements. Their menfolk are usually keen on upholding a blend of local customs and religious principles that have traditionally preserved their prerogatives over wives and daughters, if not women in the community at large.

Agency and Fear

To return to conviction as motivation for donning the hijab, it seems as illusive as modesty. What is it that a woman is convinced about? Is it that the hijab is a pillar of Islam? It is not. Is it that the hijab unambiguously signifies commitment to a Muslim ethic? It does not. Nowhere in the Quran is there an indication that the veil is a condition of a woman's acceptance of her faith. I am reminded of a young Asian American woman who converted to Islam in 2001. She was told to wear a headscarf, and she enthusiastically complied. But a few weeks later she came to see me in tears. She candidly talked about her fears and worries at the unexpectedly bounded life that had become hers. She had joined a Muslim group in the city, where she was told to keep watch on what foot to put forward when she enters a room, which hand to use in opening a door, how she should turn her head, and such details of body comportment. She was the mother of a baby girl and felt that she could not keep track of gestures and movements that she used to make mechanically but had now become the center of her life, taking attention away from other pressing concerns, such as caring for her baby and working. Life had become difficult for her when she expected it to bring her spiritual comfort. She asked whether all Muslims had to mind their every gesture at all times. She also asked whether a moment of forgetfulness that would cause her to use the wrong hand in opening a door would mean that she had committed a sin! Her questions filled me with extreme sadness at the distorted way in which Islam had been presented to this young convert. It also filled me with dread at the realization that various practices centered on the body, many of which, originating in unreliable hadiths disseminated in how-to booklets for Muslims, had become part of the ostensibly pious trend that has swept through the Muslim world and Western countries.

This young convert's experience was painful. She had sought support in joining the group but was met with a barrage of trivial details that confused and scared her. She needed encouragement, a warm embrace, and enlightenment about her new faith, not a mindless formalism, superstitions, and an obsessive concern with the body. Yet such superstitions play a role in the configuration of reasons for which many women are turning to the hijab. The case of Rabi'a, a twenty-year-old bright and self-possessed woman, is one in point. She was born to a Muslim family from South Asia who came to the United States when she was a child. Her mother and older sister wear the hijab, but she feels that they did not pressure her to follow their example. Rabi'a prayed daily but did not take up the hijab until the spring of 2008. She had had the hijab on her mind since junior high school. Her mother frequently read to her daughters from the hadith about "religion not about the veil." After she took up the hijab, Rabi'a reported that her mother was pleased yet worried about whether this was just a passing fad for her daughter. Her father was agreeably surprised and complimented her on her beauty, which he felt had been enhanced by the headscarf. She did look different with her head wrapped in layers of sequined silk that flattered the oval of her subtly made up face.

Rabi'a discussed a number of factors that culminated in her decision to don a headscarf and discard her jeans for a long skirt (at times she also wore baggy pants that did not "show the shape of the body" or a loose skirt over her old jeans). She made what she believed to be an informed decision. She had attended lectures by instructors (some of whom were imams) teaching at Al Maghrib Institute, a "self-accredited bachelor's program" providing classes in a six-day, two weekend seminar format, using "exciting new teaching methods." Some of the instructors are imams from abroad, others are trained lecturers from the United States who had graduated from Islamic universities in Medina (Saudi Arabia) as well as Al Azhar in Cairo; they all lecture throughout the United States.[9] She had also attended a lecture by rapper Napoleon, who is a convert to Islam, as well as two talks on a variety of topics, including the veil and Muslim women's rights. Although her family may have predisposed her to eventually wearing the hijab, Rabi'a made an informed decision. After she changed her dress, she felt as though "a weight had been lifted off my shoulders." She argued that "we're going to answer to Allah for it [the hijab]" and that "it's up to Allah to punish us." Asked what punishment she would have incurred if she had not worn the hijab, she revealed that her mother as well as her sister had told her that "if a man sees one strand of your hair, your hair turns into a big snake biting you after you die." I wondered out loud whether she believed this to be true, but she did not flinch. She knew that this information was not in the Quran, just as she emphatically pointed out that "my faith could be the size of an atom, even though I am dressed like this." She intimated by this that a veil does not increase a woman's faith any more than its absence would make a woman faithless. Yet she also argued that faith needs to be expressed "in your acts." Wearing the hijab is acting out one's faith; it "represents your faith."

Rabi'a is an educated, not illiterate, person. Yet she could talk about the snake superstition with a straight face and had in the end decided to don a hijab in light of it. The cognitive dissonance between mythical and rational thought, faith in God and superstition, was bridged by the assertion of a feeling of wholeness that she experienced now that she had taken up the hijab. Headscarf and loose pants reconciled the irreconcilable, covering over the contradictory nature of her statements that she was fulfilling her obligation to God, acting out her faith in God, yet invoking the bites of mythical snakes as the consideration that ultimately tipped the balance for her. Not only is the image of hair turning into a snake frightening, it also powerfully reminds a woman that her body is the source and cause of damnation; there is a medusa lurking in it. Because of her hair a woman can and will incur a most gruesome torture. That this is alien to the Quranic exhortation which only focused on bosoms and pudenda need not be reiterated. It is unclear to me why a headscarf would ward off a snake lurking in one's grave. It is the very existence of a woman's hair that gives this imaginary snake the opportunity to materialize. Getting rid of one's hair altogether would be just as good a protection from this hellish reptile as a headscarf.

In retrospect, Assia, the young woman who had shaved her head, may have unwittingly resolved the medusa problem.

One could argue that Rabi'a's case is unique and that for most women who turned to the hijab, superstition played little or no role at all. However, discussions I held with women from Turkey reveal that the same superstition is invoked by a number of those who opted for a head covering. Rabi'a's story sheds new light on the complexity of the concept of conviction. It means not only doing right by God, but also fearing retribution. Interestingly, conviction regarding the veil in this case appears to be a function of punishment, and the certainty of punishment is not derived from God's word but from superstition. And because this superstition focuses on women's hair and women's hair only, it denotes intent to scare women into submitting to the hijab where religious arguments may not be strong enough to sway them. Indeed, Rabi'a was not engaged in a discussion of the relevant suras of the Quran that address women's dress. She knew of their existence but simply assumed that they mandated the hijab. She found further reason to wear it in a hadith, the origin of which she could not identify, according to which "the Prophet and his wives described for us the way to cover." Although it is true that Prophet Muhammad's wives had taken up the hijab, they did so not for religious but for mundane reasons: the veil distinguished them from the wives and daughters of ordinary Muslims. Rabi'a had not read the Quran. She had, however, read a primer on Islam (with practice questions) by Ghulam Sarwar that included a chapter on the family, marriage, divorce, and women, and one on "Three Great Women," the first and third wives of the Prophet as well as his first daughter, Fatima. The book makes frequent historical comparisons between Muslim and Western women, showing the former to be better off than the latter.[10] The author lists women's basic "rights" in an accurate yet selective manner as if to highlight a quid pro quo that, in return for these "rights," a woman should wear a veil.

> Man and woman are not exactly equal in Islam. They have different physical and biological features. Islam recognizes the leadership of a man over a woman (4:34, 2:228) [numbers of relevant suras in the Quran] but that does not mean domination. . . . Women tend to be sensitive, emotional and tender while men are comparatively less emotional. . . . Throughout history, men and women have never been treated the same. Islam has given women the right position and has not attempted to violate divine laws. Other religions and philosophies have failed to define the exact and appropriate role of women. In the West, women have been reduced almost to a plaything of enjoyment and fancy. Women have tended to degrade themselves probably unwittingly in modern times for the sake of real or imaginary equality. They have become objects of exploitation by men and the slogan of liberty and equality has virtually reduced them to playful commodities. They have neither gained liberty nor achieved full equality; rather they have lost their natural place in the home. The natural balance, fairness and mutuality have been disturbed. The outcome has been horrendous for social peace and stability. The natural peace at home should be restored.[11]

I will return to the use of the role of the "West" in the thought of male advocates of veiling in my last letter. It is important to note that reference to Western women in this text is intended to reconcile women born to Muslim communities to their presumed naturally inferior condition, described as biologically inscribed, rule-bound, and ordained by religion. One of the Prophet's wives whom the author lists as admirable for her model behavior, Aisha, had led an army in opposition to Ali the fourth Caliph, successor to her husband. Yet, although the book applauds her intelligence and education, it also emphasizes that she "loved and enjoyed serving her husband. She used to do the household work, including grinding flour and baking bread. She would make the beds and do the family washing."[12] A more truthful account would have extolled her independent spirit and her stepping into the political fray and out of her household chores. There are many such books sold throughout the Muslim world and in countries with Muslim immigrants. They introduce people in many languages to the essential principles of their religion. However, in recent years they have specifically targeted women for selective information about their "rights" and obligations under Islam, providing them with arguments with which to counter Western critiques of women's roles in Muslim societies. Although they correct some of the misconceptions that uninformed people have of Islam, these books and lectures also create new ones. Specialized books, manuals, as well as regular talks and crash courses on Islam are a critical part of young women's decision to don a hijab. Echoing Sarwar's argument that husbands' power over wives means complementarity, not dominance, Rabi'a told me that "the Quran gives us equal rights with our husbands. Western women say that we have no rights, yet God gave us rights. We do not need a Susan B. Anthony; we do not need a movement. We have the right to inheritance; we get to keep our money which a son does not. We have more rights than men."

Exchange of information through email constitutes an additional source of knowledge about and support for the hijab. It is through the Internet that Rabi'a learned how to dress appropriately, how to avoid "tight fitting and see-through clothes." Ironically, it is through YouTube videos of a non-Muslim young woman, Shayla, that she also learned several methods of wrapping the scarf around her head. Shayla, a pretty American woman, demonstrates several ways of tying the scarf and what to put under it (a head band or a sock hat) to prevent it from slipping, as well as how to make room for dangling earrings. More interestingly, she explains how she took up the hijab although she is not a Muslim. Defining herself as a spiritual woman tired of the Western obsession with sex and the "imbalanced American culture," she felt that the hijab offers "protection from unwanted looks," in addition to being a source of "beauty." The hijab in her estimation also protects her skin from polluting chemicals. She recommends it to any woman who feels "oppressed" by bare midriffs and shorts. She nevertheless reminds her viewers that a woman must examine her motivations before donning the hijab—an odd comment for a non-Muslim woman to make as it denotes a concern for the significance of faith in taking up the hijab.[13]

In spite of Shayla's rejection of unwanted men's looks, her hijab demonstration is fraught with seductiveness. She coquettishly admires herself in a mirror and moves her face into the camera for a close-up of her eyes. Whether these videos are genuine or the work of a paid actress is not immediately clear. Shayla pointedly stresses that no one put her up to them. Yet her monologue seems to indicate that she is well connected with Muslim groups, and not a mere observer who happened to fall in love with the hijab. Ultimately, the answer does not matter; what does is the fact that the valuation of the hijab has entered a proselytizing social discourse and representations of women. By proselytizing I do not mean that the hijab in and of itself is an instrument of proselytism. Rather, it is emerging as a tool for engaging women in a conception of religiosity that serves the political aims of various groups scattered throughout the Muslim world, who are eager to demonstrate the success and reach of their views. The organized character of the revival of the hijab needs to be emphasized as it raises doubts about a number of justifications offered by women for veiling.

I do not question Rabi'a's faith. I believe it is genuine. However, the context of information, knowledge-sharing, and a support network inflects its meaning and undermines its significance. The materials she read, the lectures she attended, the Internet sites she used were biased in favor of the hijab. Besides, although she sought to inform herself before making a decision, she did not read original sources. Her case is instructive because it casts the issue of agency in a different light. By all counts Rabi'a's decision was the outcome of deliberate choice. Yet her "choice" was constrained by the informational context within which it was made. Her family, important as it was, was not the sole motivating factor in her decision; it was complemented by the information Rabi'a gathered with the help of her sister. Because of her family, in her estimation, she made a decision sooner than she would normally have. But it is the organized network of "experts," lecturers in religious matters, cultural brokers of sorts, linking immigrant communities in the United States with their own organizations and with Muslim countries that integrated Rabi'a in a larger circle of women and men loosely connected to one another by their common religion. This frame of reference reinforced her family's influence on her. Rabi'a felt empowered to speak about "rights" in Islam and dismiss women's movements in the West as symbolizing Western women's de facto oppression. She did not question the selectivity of the information she received, truly fearing that her hair might turn into snakes if she did not cover it.

If agency signifies acting under one's own power, it follows that Rabi'a's decision to don the hijab was that of a free agent. But if agency means making decisions in full knowledge of one's motivations and the consequences of one's acts, after weighing the pros and cons and considering alternatives, then Rabi'a's choice was not free. There is not enough space in this letter to engage in a philosophical discussion of the differences between free will and agency, or whether will is ever free. Nevertheless, and even though Rabi'a's case may not be representative, it clearly demonstrates that conviction is as shaky a justification of veiling as convenience, or pleasing one's husband. To be convincing, conviction would require that a woman provide arguments for veiling that would be on a par with Islam's basic tenet of the unicity and undivided oneness of God that permits no gender double standard.[14] In other words, it would be an argument that does not rest on the snake superstition, but one according to which God ordained a double standard of worship, one for men and the other for women, in violation of the constitutive principle of Islam. But this is a claim that the staunchest advocates of veiling would be unwilling to make, as it would contradict a tenet of Islam that women and men are equal in their duties and obligations to their maker, which in reality do not include veiling.

Rabi'a's case further illustrates the difficulty of ascertaining a woman's decision to don the hijab in an international climate saturated with the revival of old customs, many of which are imbued with religious meaning. Unlike Qama,

Rabi'a categorically denied that politics, or making a political statement, had any role in her decision. She admitted in a resigned way that she had now become conspicuous on the street and in the subway system. But she said, "It does not bother me; I do not worry about it." She felt "more plenitude" under the hijab than without it. I cannot argue with a woman's feelings; they matter. I do question the process and framework that gave rise to them and nurtured them. Conviction does not remove the purely mundane factor in the decision to wear the hijab. When asked, Rabi'a said that she thought that her chances of marrying may have improved. This was meant to explain the added benefit of complying with what she believes to be a religious obligation.

At times, conviction is synonymous with a resigned acceptance of the inevitability of the veil. Safya, a young woman of twenty-two from a South Asian immigrant family to New York, explained that "you cannot pick and choose. If you are a Muslim you have to assume your religion in its entirety; you have to wear the hijab." This categorical statement was not based on an informed judgment. Safya assumed that her duty as a Muslim was to wear a hijab. I took her comment to mean that she was unhappy about her tightly wrapped black headscarf and long dress, but Islam is the religion she grew up in and liked, and as a result she felt that she had to endure the veil. Yet as a Muslim she could also have availed herself of the Islamic principle that religion cannot be a burden and abstained from wearing the veil.

Conviction as Visibility

Rabi'a's itinerary is similar to that of young women born to immigrant families in France, although the meaning attached to the veil may differ. France has a long history of involvement in Muslim countries, not the least of which is Algeria, where the colonial French government did not extend full citizenship rights to Algerians until 1958 because of their religion. Second-generation immigrants whose parents hail from North Africa encounter cultural prejudices similar to those experienced by Algerians during the colonial era. As citizens, France is their home, and thus they find it difficult to tolerate exclusion as did their parents or grandparents, had who hoped to return to their country of origin sooner or later. Many, women as well as men, fight endemic prejudice against their culture by stressing their Muslim identity (heretofore kept invisible) by joining groups affiliated with transnational faith-based organizations, or empower themselves with their French citizenship to stake a claim for a different French identity grounded in an assertive Muslim traditional ethic. Just like Rabi'a, a number of French women turned to books and conferences on Islam to inform themselves about a culture with which they were somewhat familiar because it was their parents', but the history of which eluded them, as well as the role played in it by Islam. In this way, they discovered a face of Islam that some parents, locked in the isolation of immigrant life, failed to reveal to them except in the form of a defensive and rigid assertion of their right to save their daughters from adopting the lifestyles of non-Muslim French women. There are also parents who, eager to assimilate into French society, avoided discussions of religion in bringing up their children. Needless to say, the educational system in France had also failed to enlighten these women about the richness of their parents' culture or respect it as part of a universal fund of human values. Consequently, a number of women felt that after reflecting on their marginalization, they achieved religious "conviction" and donned the hijab.

It took two years for Sabrina to decide to veil herself. Her quest for meaning is similar to Rabi'a's:

> I found myself in a schizophrenic situation: on the one hand, I felt a profound need to veil myself; on the other hand, I knew that people's perceptions of me would change. When I got out during the day, I was not concerned about the veil but when I got back home at night I had to face myself and felt uncomfortable; there was only God and I.... I felt that I had to choose between God and society.... The veil is truly obligatory. At first, you don't want it to be obligatory. I was convinced that it was when I realized that God spoke about it to all the prophets before Muhammad, to Moses (peace be on him), to Jesus (pbh).... the message is truly divine.[15]

Sabrina found that wearing a veil in France is a manner of "advocating for Islam," to make it visible and likable—a sentiment also shared by Turkish women in hijab.[16] Consequently, she undertook to wear cheerful colors instead of the black frequently worn by veiled women.[17] It will be noted in passing that Sabrina's decision as she recounts it responded to a felt need to be in accordance with what she perceived to be God's command. She does not explain what sources she used to arrive at this conclusion. However, as with other French women, she turned to the veil in a society that is contemptuous of Islam and had been engulfed in a media campaign in the 1990s that assaulted the dignity of millions of citizens who identify with Islam in one way or another. Her constant references to "others," her worry that they would change their attitudes toward her, cast a shadow on Sabrina's turn to the veil. Had she lived in a society free of anti-Muslim prejudice, she probably would not have felt the need to "advocate" for Islam. Hostility, like persecution, breeds determination to defend its object.

Like Sabrina, Saïda argues that wearing the veil fulfills two important functions: a display of "humility" before God and *visibility* to her faith. However, Saïda, very active in the movement to bring an end to other forms of discrimination against French Muslims, sees her turn to the veil as a way of "reminding [man] that a woman is a human being like him. 'Remember that she is your equal and thus deserves your respect.'"[18] Conviction in her case is tangled up with two very mundane pursuits: gain respect from Muslim men and oppose (illegal) discrimination against women who wear a hijab at work. This instrumental use of the veil is problematic for two reasons. First, it legitimizes the veil—a custom that transcends France and French Muslims—by using it as a cultural weapon for the expansion of civil rights. Second, it presents the use of the veil as a *right* conflated with freedom of religion. The right to wear the veil is used as the right to live by one's religious principles. In other words, female advocates of veiling wish to make the veil stand for religion and in so doing close the uncertainty and indeterminacy of the religious status of the veil. They thus lend virtual support to the state policies that mandate veiling in countries such as Iran and Saudi Arabia. Conviction, a personal matter, becomes for French Muslim women a public claim to a purportedly new way of being French, an alternative to the aggressive and inconsistent conception of secularism or *laïcité*. In a display of a blend of contempt for the generation of their parents (who "prayed in cellars") and amnesia for the layered history of the veil, female advocates of veiling claim to have developed a new conception of Islam that is "de-ethnicized" insofar as it is part of a demand for acceptance of Muslims as French citizens, rather than members of a (religious) minority group inside the French nation.

Young Muslim French women, just like their Turkish counterparts, wish to distinguish themselves from older generations of women throughout the Middle East and North Africa whom they perceive as having worn the veil passively, out of habit. By contrast, they see themselves as actively engaged in a process of reclaiming their religion and defending it armed with the appropriate knowledge. Generational conflicts aside, I must confess my skepticism at this justification of the veil. On the one hand, the lives of older women such as my mother and her mother are dismissed in the same manner as the Turkish state or the French state has dismissed veiled women; on the other hand, the veil—the very same veil that women have always worn—is singled out as the most significant sign of the newly reclaimed religion. I would have expected this younger generation of women to come up with a new way by which to identify their religiosity. I am afraid that they have unwittingly linked up with my grandmother's generation. She too was very proud of being veiled and defended the use of the veil against me, her granddaughter. She too had informed herself about her religion by attending discussions of her faith with Sufi masters and was also a valued member of a Sufi (mystical) order of the Qadiryia. The young Algerian women who believe that their mothers and grandmothers had not worn veils because they had been influenced by French anti-Muslim colonial ideology make a mistake similar to that of their French and Turkish counterparts, in addition to being uninformed about the history of Algerian women. It is true, nevertheless, that by looking into the religious texts, female advocates of veiling may find that some of their parents' religious notions are in fact erroneous.[19] They have been able to engage in patterns of interaction with Muslim men that appear "new" in France because they are different from French norms, but that are actually similar to those that have also emerged in countries such as Algeria. What is claimed as the product of French Muslim women's "agency" is in reality shared by others, and with regular exchange between Algeria and France, it is not difficult to make out the contours of the forces that shape both agency and piety.[20]

Empathy for veiled French or Turkish women's plight should not excuse them for selecting the veil as *the* sign of Muslim identity. It is difficult to see how the veil can be a constitutive part of citizenship, as has been claimed. It is as frivolous as arguing for the constitutional right to not eat pork or drink alcohol. Protection of the right to practice one's religion does not mean the right to legitimize the veil as *standing for* religion. Since the religious status of the veil is still undetermined, law cannot legitimize it one way or another, positively by mandating it, or negatively by banning it. The politicization of the veil on all sides obscures this seldom-recognized detail. The veil is not a substantive right, just as its prohibition by law lacks compelling substantiation.[21] This said, discrimination against women who wear a veil in the workplace is a violation of their right to work. Law should not interfere in the matter of veiling, except to ensure that women in veils are not the objects of discrimination. Ironically, in protecting the right to be free of discrimination, the law implicitly protects the "right" of a woman to wear the veil. No woman should derive satisfaction from this, especially if she considers its implication for the girl-child who would grow up with the understanding that the veil is a "right." It would have been a victory for all Muslim women if the French or Turkish states had been brought to task for making the veil stand for religion. The veil is a matter for women to come to terms with, to *de-mystify*, and to relentlessly work toward making redundant. Although national context is an important factor to keep in mind in making sense of the meaning attached to reveiling by Muslim as well as non-Muslim women, it is equally important to place the veil in its proper perspective lest one becomes complicit with its proponents.

There is little that is substantively new about reveiling. And the young women who take up the hijab are no pioneers. In fact in the time warp that the veil effectuates, they are my grandmother's virtual contemporaries. Had they become the architects of a new conception of social change centered on women, or found a way of making problematic texts related to veiling redundant, they would have indeed earned their claim as innovators. But they have not; the veil remains an issue.

In the end, conviction when used as a political instrument to fight for the "right" to be veiled is harmful to the women who look for respect outside of a quasi-religious custom. Furthermore, it should not obscure the fact that a number of young French women resigned themselves to the hijab in order to put an end to battering by a father or brother, or sexual harassment in a ghetto, and to be able to go to school in peace. Houria, a twenty-five-year-old French woman, spoke about growing up in a dysfunctional immigrant family with an unemployed father and a wayward older brother who took to beating her until the day she decided to wear the hijab: "I woke up one morning sore from the beatings I received the night before and felt like a veil. I put on the veil with mechanical gestures as if I had always worn it. Yet I rarely prayed with my mother. Between homework, running errands and house chores, I had no time for much else. But that morning, I had a sudden need for the veil." After this act, she noticed a radical change in her brother, who began to take credit for her newly acquired virtue. "All that they [father, brother, and brother's friends] retained was that I straightened myself up on the day that I wore the veil, as if *I* had been the problem! But I keep quiet because thanks to God I have become free. Every day, I pray for this to continue."[22] She can now keep up with her vocational courses.

The French environment, weighed down by an unresolved colonial past, biases an assessment of the meaning of conviction and piety. Nevertheless, what advocates of veiling perceive as putting their mark on French Islam is misleading at best. But it is theorized and supported by male advocates of the veil, such as Tariq Ramadan, a rising theologian, who, like the men who lecture American Muslim women about their rights and duties, provides tantalizing arguments for developing a purely European Muslim identity that in effect integrates women in the same culture of the veil that embraced my mother and grandmother.[23] I will be returning to him in my last letter. At first glance there is nothing unusual about imams preaching about religion. Christian priests do the same in France and elsewhere. What is of concern is imams' deliberate intent to define women as special carriers of religious morality. As a formerly colonized woman, I am at once intrigued and bemused by the value placed on the veil as a means of achieving respect by French society. I went to a French public high school where the administration did not wince when a classmate entered the school grounds in a veil (the niqab) every day. It is true that she took it off in class on her own, for her own convenience. A battle for the veil can only lead to a pyrrhic victory. And it may in the end be a passing phase in a society troubled by its diversity.[24]

In closing this letter, I will note that justifications of the hijab are seldom, if ever, preceded by a discussion of alternatives to veiling. Women I spoke to do not identify what is wrong with not wearing the hijab or wearing clothes of decent length that do not expose one's breasts. Nor do they seem to be aware that using makeup when wearing a hijab may be a violation of the injunction that women "not reveal their adornments," assuming that these—and they are a matter of both translation and interpretation—are enhanced by eyeliner and lipstick. A woman's piety can no more be ensured by the hijab than her looks determine her character. To argue otherwise is to reduce faith, a personal matter of conscience, to a formal display of evidentiary signs designed to reassure *others*, men and the community, that a woman is indeed a convinced and pious Muslim. This clearly opens wide the door to deception and simulation of piety that make it more difficult to distinguish authenticity from acting. That male advocates of the veil are not bothered by this but are satisfied by the outer signs of piety is an indication that their goals are not to promote women's spiritual needs, but to increase the material visibility of Islam through the hijab at the expense of both women and their religion. Indeed, seeing a veiled woman for these men is more comforting than advocating for social justice or equality. Their vision of a neatly ordered world in which women and men occupy different and fixed spaces is vindicated. Besides, the hijab shores up their self-identity as males. There seems to be nothing like a hijab to symbolize more tangibly and palpably the putatively natural inequality between men and women. The hijab materializes the gap between the two. The greater the gap, the more crystallized identity becomes. It is comforting for a man to see a woman in a hijab, just as it is reassuring for a woman to be in a hijab. The identity lines are drawn clearly and unmistakably. No man would wear a hijab of his free will. But a man makes sure that a woman wears it of her "free" will and makes it part of herself, as happened with my mother and her friends long ago. Consequently, the veil is not just a dress that a woman puts on and takes off to make a point; it is not just a garment, no matter what name it goes by. A woman who wears it cannot claim equality. One cannot be on both sides of the veil equation.

LETTER FIVE
Why Women Should Not Wear the Veil

My previous letters have shown how justifications for wearing the veil are often more mundane than religious. There are a number of reasons why women should not wear a veil. These include the need to recapture the historic role that women have played as agents of change; doing away with the physical and psychological effects of veiling; awareness of the effect of the veil in the workplace; and demystifying propaganda that portrays women's desire for progress as mimicry of the "West" and thus an offense to their culture and religion.

Obligation to History

The history of Muslim societies is fraught with instances when women wore no veil without there being much ado. The veil rose and fell depending on local political circumstances. Its evolution mirrored women's changed perceptions of themselves. The way my mother thought of herself at the time of the incident in which she involuntarily hurt me in trying to help me had changed by the time she had decided to shed her veil. In the intervening years, the Algerian war had seen the participation of many women in combating colonial injustice. At the independence of their country, women, in large numbers, did not wear the veil. Naturally, many continued to tend to their religious duties, praying and fasting during Ramadan. The veil had lost the religious meaning with which it had been imbued during the colonial era and was understood as a custom suited for the older generation of women, mothers and grandmothers, who had not received a formal education. These were the women who had reared the men and women that took up arms against France. Gradually, the veil also became a sign of social class: the new maids who served the emerging postcolonial dominant classes (political as well as professional) were generally poor women who seemed to hide their poverty in their veils. Accepted as a remnant of the past for the generation made redundant by history, the veil was looked down upon as an archaic custom, devoid of substantive meaning. No wonder women like my mother decided to discard it. They were eager to evade the new class stigma and experience the freedom to move about, unswaddled by their silky white sheets. There were, to be sure, men who objected to the occasional young woman who ventured out in a miniskirt, but by and large women could go to college or work without a veil. The religious establishment in the 1960s and 1970s condemned prostitution but was more occupied with the socialist policy of land expropriation and redistribution, which it opposed, than with the veiling of women.

The current revival of the veil, often in a style imported from Egypt (a headscarf and long overcoat) coincided with a failed development policy, a civil war that pitted the government against a radical and splintered Islamist movement, and the emergence of an intraregional movement of cultural identity inflected by geopolitical events. What goes on in Baghdad and Cairo, Washington, D.C., and Paris, has resonance in Algiers, Rabat, or Amman. In the history of domination, resistance, and protest in Middle Eastern societies, the veil has been an enduring symbol and fertile ground for dramatizing political ideologies. French military officers engaged in an elaborate propaganda battle seeking to win women to their side. They dramatically unveiled a group of women in public in 1958, thus turning the veil into a symbol of colonial assault on the native people's culture and beliefs.[1] Thirty-four years later, a fractious Islamist movement used various means of coercion to compel women to take up the hijab. Ironically, one of the women who fought French troops, arms in hand, Louisette Ighilahriz, came under pressure in the mid-1990s from women in her neighborhood to "at least put on a headscarf!"

In Iran, a number of women wore the veil in protest against the shah's repressive policies in the 1970s. As soon as Khomeini came to power, he returned women's favor by mandating the veil. Like an army regulation, a decree prescribed the color ("black, dark blue, brown, or dark grey") of the hijab, the kind of shoes to wear, and, as a nod to choice, posted pictures of "accepted" and "preferred" dress under the caption "Pattern of Islamic Hijab."[2] It is worth noting that the Iranian opposition movement, the Mujahedin-e Khalq, created a National Liberation Army in the late 1990s in which women recruits fought alongside Iraq (during the Iran–Iraq War) wearing bright red headscarves.[3] It is true that the Iranian Revolutionary Guards wear stylized turbans, but they at least have their foreheads and necks free. Like Saudi Arabia, Iran has vice and virtue police who search for wayward women who might trifle with veil regulations.

The state supervision and control of women's dress and bodies is not only humiliating but also inhumane. No man has the right to dictate to a woman what color or length of dress she should wear. This is the most blatant abuse of power. Yet, by contrast, Mr. Ahmadinejad, the president of the Islamic Republic of Iran, travels to Western countries dressed like a Western man. The virtue and vice police do not object to his dress, and no one would think him less Muslim for not wearing a long robe and turban. Why should his adoption of non-Muslim dress carry no penalty when a woman can be arrested for allowing a strand of hair to show from her headscarf? What is the justice in this? If men are free to dress the way they wish, so should women.

Unlike religious prescriptions pertaining to dogma, the veil is a historical, if not the most historical, exhortation and therefore amenable to change.[4] It carries no heretical connotation or penalty. Going out without it is not a prohibition, as usury or drinking alcohol is. This explains why nineteenth-century Muslim reformists called for improvements in women's social lives—largely held back by veiling. However, even the most liberal among them fell short of declaring the veil a nonreligious practice in its essence. In 1879 Jamal ad-Din al-Afghani warned his contemporaries "that you should not ignore that it is impossible for us to emerge from stupidity, from the prison of humiliation and distress, and the depths of weakness and ignominy as long as women are deprived of rights and ignorant of their duties, for they are the mothers from whom will come elementary education and primary morality."[5] Al-Afghani's advocacy of change was not dictated by a new vision of women's future but by their role as mothers. He shied away from determining the religious status of the veil. Instead, he too imbued it with a moral function. By contrast, Qasim Amin, the Egyptian jurist and contemporary of Al-Afghani, found no compelling reason in religion or in Islamic law for the style of veil that covers a woman's face, hands, and feet. Reading his careful treatise on *The Liberation of Women* provides grounds for the removal of the veil that covers a woman's face. It is ironic that the arguments Amin used against his male contemporaries are applicable today to women advocates of the veil—an indication of how little progress has been made on this issue. Amin pointed out the use of religion as an excuse for perpetuating a custom that was socially harmful to women. As he forcefully put it, "Muslims were attracted to the use of the veil, approved it, exaggerated its use, and dressed it up in religious raiment, just as other harmful customs have become firmly established in the name of religion, but of which religion is innocent."[6] But his impassioned demonstration of the social harm that the veil causes the Muslim family and nation notwithstanding, Amin wrote: "I still defend the use of the veil and consider it one of the permanent cornerstones of morality."[7] Nevertheless, Amin, unlike many women who have veiled themselves, evinced sensitivity to the impact of veiling on the pubescent girls of his time whose growth becomes "stunted" as a result of the enforced prohibition against interacting with the outside world as soon as they wear the veil.[8] The veil thus constitutes the limit of the liberalism of reformist thought. It is up to women today to make the next step and put an end to the politics of the veil by simply not wearing it as many women did in the 1950s and 1960s. It is women's obligation to history to forge ahead as agents of social change and complete the work started by the previous generation.

Glorification of the veil overlooks the existential experience of women who have from generation to generation been socialized into concealing their bodies and made the veil part of their persona, as happened with my mother. Rehabilitation of the veil cannot dispense with a hard look at the subversion and transformation of the meanings of the veil, ranging from a tool of confinement to one of purported liberation. The long, dark blue, billowing Afghan dress, the Algerian white veil, the black Iranian chador, and the ubiquitous open-face hijab all speak to a history in which men watched over women's dutiful discharge of their roles as guardians of their sexual domain. That some men have a romantic view of the veil is beyond doubt. The veil is the most visible common denominator of Muslim societies. Men seeking to hark back to an age when society appeared simpler because it was well ordered, in which every member had a predefined role and function and women did not openly question their status, find in the veil more than religious virtue. It is a marker of their uncontested social status. It is as if, without it, their identity were incomplete, left in abeyance, in wait for substantiation and recognition. It is thrilling for a young man to have his will carried out in spite of resistance when his sister, mother, or girlfriend complies with his insistence that she wear a veil. Some young men stipulate in the marriage contract what kind of veil their brides should wear. A young Algerian man now working in France made sure that his fiancée, left behind in his hometown, put on a jilbab (previously unknown to Algeria), a long dress that sweeps the ground as a woman walks, face bare but head ensconced in a fitted garment that falls over the shoulders or waist, gloves, and socks. This modern version of the medieval chastity belt illustrates the entanglement of the veil in men's identity. In France, the groom-to-be wears shorts, works out in a gym, visits a neighborhood mosque, and on occasion flirts with a French woman. His masculinity is grounded in and feeds on the obliteration of his fiancée's existence as a social being. This is hardly a unique case.

Physical Inconvenience

It is undeniable that wearing a tightly wrapped scarf on the head secured in place by an underlying headband or skullcap makes the head sweat in hot weather. Is this any different from the old tradition (now all but relinquished) among men in North Africa of wearing an intricate turban over a tall and round *shesh*, secured in place with a long black or red cord? For these men the headdress was part of a costume, just like a top hat was for an Englishman. North African men also changed their headdress with the seasons. In the summer they would remove the intricate structure and substitute for it a lighter turban around their heads, leaving their ears free. For women, the headscarf is expected. Years ago I traveled by bus in early July between the cities of Wahran and Algiers. A passenger sitting behind me kept opening the window for air, causing others to complain about the dust that the hot wind blew in. When I looked back, I saw that it was a woman wearing a white veil. She was leaning forward against the back of my seat, face dripping with pearly sweat, using the sides of her veil as a fan while making sure that the man sitting next to her did not see her face. I felt uneasy at her discomfort. There we were, both Muslim women, but she was silently and unnecessarily suffering more than I from the heat.

The veiled women I grew up with, including my mother, frequently complained about the heat trapped in their full white veils. The women wearing black veils, socks, and gloves suffer even more, as the black color absorbs the heat of the sun instead of reflecting it. The Afghan burqa, which covers the face with its gridlike woven pane, and the niqab, which leaves only a slit for the eyes, are equally inconvenient in hot weather, in addition to being difficult to manage: the long dress usually bunches up against and between the legs, preventing a woman from taking long steps or running. That some young women have swapped pants for long skirts is a sign of recognition of this problem. They do not realize, however, that their clothing contradicts the logic of the veil (to which they have subscribed), that the veil sets a woman apart from a man, starting with the manner in which she dresses. Rabi'a, the newly veiled woman discussed in letter 4, felt the need to wear her old tight-fitting jeans under a flouncy skirt that fell below her knee to retain part of her former persona before she took up the hijab. The various styles of putting a veil together betray awareness of the difficulty of combining this custom with the physical freedom required by the bustle of modern life in a city.

On a subway platform in New York, I recently came upon a young woman wearing sneakers, a long denim skirt, a denim jacket, a layered scarf, and a long black muslin cloth that covered her nose, mouth, and neck, falling nearly to her waist. Her headscarf was set low over her forehead, almost touching the top of the muslin on her nose bridge. She carried a black canvas bag stamped with the words "Young Muslims." Her eclectic veil combined the comfort of modern accoutrement with the uncomfortable remnants of the old style of veiling. This being New York, not Paris, no one even glanced at this anonymous woman. Yet the purpose of her dress assemblage was to give her visibility as a symbol of the presence of her religion in the midst of the frenzied urban crowd. But the visibility of her veil managed to obliterate her as a person. This use of anonymity as presence hardly drove the point home to the unconcerned crowd waiting for the next train that Islam is a great religion, or that it is here to stay. If it was meant as a gesture of provoking interest in Islam, the eclectic veil failed its purpose. In the end no one cared; the anonymous woman passed unnoticed. Undoubtedly, some passengers had personal opinions on what they saw, and some, at another station, might even have voiced a comment. But, by and large, the anonymous woman's garb was for many just one more sign of social diversity in a multi-ethnic metropolis. Nevertheless, I could imagine how she must have felt when she boarded a crowded train, cheek to jowl with strangers, each pushing and shoving in a sweaty atmosphere, with perhaps her muslin slipping off her face. A veil is neither comfortable nor convenient.

Perception, Self, and Meaning

Perhaps a more compelling reason for not wearing a veil is its unrecognized psychological effect on its wearer. In the long run, a hijab makes a woman feel removed from her environment. There is a simple explanation to this drawback: a piece of cloth that covers the ears several hours a day blunts sensory perception. As it is worn throughout the day, the hijab is more physically constraining than the old-style veil, which in the past was worn only outside the house and for relatively brief periods of time since women did not work outside their homes. The hijab may leave a woman's face uncovered, but it tightens itself on her head and ears. That some women have tried to fasten their headscarves in such a way as to leave their ears free is an acknowledgment of the hijab's effect on the sharpness of their sensory perception, notwithstanding the coquettish desire of some to make room for earrings. Conversely, the removal of a headscarf may become a source of discomfort as it is for Qama, who finds it necessary to put a band over her ears when she is at home to maintain the pressure on her head to which she has grown accustomed.

The hijab induces in its wearer a sense that biology is destiny, and destiny is making sure that the body is not seen in its contours. A woman must repress her body. However, repressing the body is tantamount to repressing the self. The self in Arabic is *nafs*, which means the mind as well as the soul. The person is one, body and mind, and when the body is defined as in need of concealment and repression, the self is affected as a result. My mother was not the only woman to have been so thoroughly socialized in the veil culture that she could not get out without it in an emergency situation. Many women of her generation felt naked without their veils. Internalizing the veil as part of selfhood is a measure of the depth of the psychological effect of veiling on a woman.

When the veil is mandated by the state, it thwarts a woman's desire for authenticity that requires a meshing of her inner life with her behavior or external life. Complying with veil laws (made by men, not God) instills in a woman a sense of helplessness, as these laws cannot be appealed; they enshrine discrimination. In countries where the veil is enforced, such as Iran and Saudi Arabia, interaction with men is severely curtailed and monitored. This makes it difficult for women (as well as men) to develop a realistic sense of the other gender. Furthermore, it leads to intricate strategies and maneuvers by young women and men who use cell phones and the Internet to circumvent law and tradition. This speaks not only to the futility of veiling, but also to the irrepressibility of the body's demands, which the veil seeks to deny. Where laws do not prevent women from meeting men, the veil (even if reduced to a headscarf) creates a psychological distance between a woman and a man. A woman does not face a man as an equal being; she faces him as a fundamentally different being whose difference must be given the symbol (the veil) of inequality. Whether a woman is convinced of the legitimacy of the veil or not, she understands that it is a symbol of gender difference that by definition is unsurpassable but manageable through concealment of the body. Consequently, consciously or unconsciously, a woman who takes up the veil accepts her essentialized difference from men (valued negatively) and gives it credence. Furthermore, she also enfolds herself in a gamut of behavior patterns stemming from the unacknowledged self-deception that veiling entails. Having paid her duty, so to speak, to the rule of body concealment, a woman may nevertheless engage in a range of behavior patterns that are in violation of one of the core functions of the veil: not to engage in sexual activity with men outside of marriage. Hence, some French Muslim women engage in *haram* or sinful behavior (such as having sexual relations with a man before marriage) for a *halal* or licit reason, namely, that the lover is the chosen future husband.[9] In other words, the character of the veil as concealment calls into being an open-ended casuistry that the individual woman (or man) uses as a matter of fact but that must remain unacknowledged as such. In this sense, the veil undermines faith. Undoubtedly the psychology of the veil affects other facets of the self. But this is an uncharted domain in which I do not wish to venture.

The psychology of the veil is not confined to Muslim women—it also affects non-Muslim women. In France, many non-Muslim women reacted with unusual verbal violence during the headscarf controversy. A French woman in a hijab was perceived as a threat (as well as affront) to a non-Muslim woman's belief in the propriety, if not superiority, of her conception of the role of sex and femininity in her life.[10] By contrast, in the United States there are women in whom the veil arouses ambivalence about their perception of themselves. They ponder whether the hijab might not be a viable alternative to the objectification and commodification of women's bodies in capitalist society. A professor of geography once told me that she found nothing objectionable about veiling. In fact, she explained that she would welcome the opportunity to wear a veil should she go to Iran or Saudi Arabia. I suspect that she, like a number of women who share her opinion, evinces a romantic view of the veil. She and others unconsciously yearn for some "protection" from the excesses of the media as well as the fashion industry's license with women's dress. Consequently, they look with benevolence upon the reveiling trend. They fail to appreciate how veiling and nudity partake in the same phenomenon: the reduction of women to their sex. If advertising in the West thrives on depictions of naked or semi-naked women, it also finds fertile ground in representations of women with hijabs in Iran. Political propaganda in Iran does not shy away from extolling the virtues of the hijab in signs displaying veiled women taking up arms to defend the Islamic Revolution, on stamps issued against "social corruption," or simply on posters that demonstrate the proper way of wearing the hijab.[11] The pictorial representation of women for political propaganda objectifies women just like advertising in Western societies does: one by covering, and the other by exposing women's bodies.

Work

The psychological effect of the veil on its wearer in the workplace is real but seldom acknowledged. The veil perpetuates the culture of gender inequality through symbolic interaction and by the same token instills in a woman an inchoate sense of her insignificance as a social being. When a working woman willingly takes up a hijab, she is telling her male colleagues, "I respect your deep-seated desire to see me covered." She is also expressing her agreement that she is inferior to them even though she may be more competent or more skilled. Since the world of work is organized on the principles of merit and competence, not gender, the hijab has the symbolic effect of diminishing the importance of formal equality in the workplace. Through the hijab, the working woman, the professional, implicitly expresses her gratitude for working alongside men and apologizes for entering a traditionally male space. This message is even more powerfully conveyed by the woman who worked for many years without a veil and decides one day to wear one. Working males may be flattered by their colleague's decision, especially in times of revivalism. They may respect her, but they also feel more empowered over her as they have been vindicated in their conception of gender inequality. A woman who wears a hijab at work contributes to a vision of social life that leads to gender segregation.

I have noticed how public offices in Algeria have gradually become segregated in the delivery of services. When I recently asked to speak to a manager, I was on several occasions directed to the office of a woman of lower rank. Once, a manager took a peek at me through his door, left ajar by his secretary as she conveyed my request to talk to him, and said, "Take her to Miss X's office; she'll take care of her." This is a trend that, if it continues, could lead to a division of office tasks according to sex instead of competence. However, the women who don the hijab at work seldom gauge the pernicious effect that their decision, no matter its motivations, can have in the long run on women's ability to achieve substantive equality in the workplace. This is not to say that a woman in a hijab should be barred from work.

I followed the trajectory of a woman inspector in a public administration. She used to be a busy professional, solving people's problems efficiently, pacing the area where the public waited with determination, listening to people's claims, directing some to the right office and waving others to follow her into her office. She was praised for her efficiency. After she took up the hijab, she was seen less frequently in the waiting area, and when her division was restructured she was passed over for promotion. Her veil may not have been the cause of her loss of advancement, but it did make her less visible as the active inspector that she had been prior to wearing it. She faded as the dynamic inspector that she had been. She complained about the excessive heat in her office, which lacked air conditioning, now that she was spending more time inside. From the perspective of her new supervisor, she was a woman in a hijab, not a talented employee to promote to a higher position. She had ceased to be an equal member of the administration; she had unknowingly removed herself from the world of competition for advancement. Yet she was a mother of two and thus in need of a raise. The hijab symbolically inserted her into a virtual domestic space. It blurred the boundary between the private and public space as they exist in a man's imaginary. A man is accustomed to seeing his older female relatives or anonymous women on the street in veils. The office space has traditionally been one in which men and women meet as legal equals. The ensuing problem of how to deal with a colleague in hijab is resolved by ignoring her as a competitor or valuable worker.

When a working woman decides to take up the hijab, she causes her male colleagues to change their perception of her. Ironically, some women think that they acquire more status, but in reality they activate in men conflicting emotions about where they stand in relation to religion, sex, and work. It is not impossible that some men may secretly be angered by a colleague who has given in to the reveiling trend. The hijab, embedded as it is in a history of gender inequality, signals to a man his superior status in the very space where his status is based on achievement, not on a presumed natural or cultural superiority. Thus gains made by women when they entered the workplace are being undermined by a transformation of a modern, merit-based bureaucracy into a neotraditional, symbolically gender-segregated environment in which the devolution of tasks is carried out according to the values of outside private interests (as, for example, those of faith-based movements).

To be recognized as *naturally* superior is not necessarily conducive to respecting the person who gave the recognition; it breeds contempt. I suspect that sexual harassment of young women at work may even increase, as a man may unconsciously like the thrill of violating the moral shield that a woman thinks she is erecting between him and her. Instead of eradicating desire or keeping it in check, the hijab at the workplace excites it further by merging the sacred with the mundane. The blurring of din (religion) and dunia (mundane life) that the hijab effectuates in the workplace harms instead of helping women in their quest for their full humanity. It must be noted that the symbolic role of the hijab in a non-Muslim workplace is different. There, a woman seeks to make her culture visible and demand that it be accommodated.

Westing the West

The "West" looms large in the compulsion to take up the hijab, whether a woman lives in a Muslim country or in Europe or North America. The West has traditionally represented a twofold challenge in the Middle East: a horizon on which to fathom or rethink one's self, and a negative limit-case, a sort of antiworld of temptations that one should worry about. Women bridge the two challenges in the minds of advocates of the veil. (I have found it intriguing that advocates of veiling, especially neofundamentalists, use the best technology Western countries can offer in promoting their views, as exemplified by the cell phone, DVDs, laptops, and the Internet. These are technologies that make readily available the very temptations that the veil is supposed to protect women from. Yet such groups wish to protect women from the West.)

Nineteenth-century reformists specifically answered the challenge of the West in a double procedure: one aimed at painstakingly showing that Islam as a religion and culture is compatible with modernity, the other acknowledging that there had been political as well as cultural problems that delayed or prevented the Muslim world from overtaking the "West." Thus incipient self-criticism was juxtaposed with the need to validate one's religious and cultural heritage. Reformists addressed the woman question (albeit without resolving it) as a measure of how bad things had become.[12] However, they had the merit of looking at their culture critically. This critical dimension has disappeared in the contemporary neofundamentalist discourse except as they blame their governments for not having abided by the Shari'a (or Islamic Law). Neofundamentalists seize upon nonveiled women as representing the allegedly decadent state in which their societies have fallen. From their perspective, returning women to the veil is at once a first step toward restoring a lost Nirvana, an act of protest as well as defiance of the "West." Loss of doubt and absolute certainty of the goodness of the old ways merge with renewed assertion of the traditional power of men over women in times of global turmoil. Remarkably, women are once more tangled up with the idea of the West. A woman who expresses freedom in her deportment is defined as one who mimics the West.

The retreat into a remote past is unabashedly framed as a defense of religion as well as retrieval of a lost identity. The West is no longer imagined as a horizon on which one could gauge the degree to which development or "rights" or "democracy" are attainable. It is the quintessential otherness that reflects the unsurpassable otherness that Islam also represents for the West. The scores are evened out. However, in this corps à corps with imagined otherness, some women have emerged as apologists instead of a *force de frappe* that seizes the opportunity to buck the tide and blaze a new trail for independence of thought and innovation. Men engaged in battles with other men have no respect for women as full-fledged human beings when they demand or expect that women wear veils as a show of support for their cause.

Solidarity based on the revival of customs that tied women down to centuries of domesticated life is no solidarity at all. It is the same old story. It would be a welcome change if these men expressed solidarity with women in their quest for recognition of their humanity as well as their capacity to decide whether their bodies are a source of shame or simple joy. When men prohibit women from wearing the hijab as a strategy with which to fight other men, they are also guilty of disrespect for women as human beings.

An Algerian Islamist once likened a veiled woman to a "moving tank."[13] Tanks evoke wars, and the veil in this man's mind is a weapon. But it is not a weapon against any real enemy except women since, in the Algerian context, the state had not prohibited the veil. The "West" was the unspoken referent of this leader's metaphor. With the veil, he implied, one could fight the enemy within, the women who did not wear it as well as the state that did not mandate it. The notion that women who shun the veil are "Westernized" is shared by advocates of the veil as well as a number of social scientists, as I described in my introduction to these letters. The referent "Westernization" implies that a woman cannot think of change outside of a Western frame of reference. It also comforts male advocates of veiling that a Muslim woman cannot but be veiled. Western people whose countries participated in the colonization of the Middle East, North Africa, and Southeast Asia may hail shunning the veil as a positive outcome of colonial or missionary ventures and pride themselves on the superiority of their cultures. In this they are as guilty as male advocates of the veil of diminishing women's achievements and struggles for social justice. They partake in the same process of objectifying women.

The West is also the object of sophisticated theological arguments in favor of the veil directed at women living in

Europe. Tariq Ramadan, the Swiss theologian of Egyptian descent, compared in the media to Martin Luther King, Jr., provides guidance to women in their quest for self-esteem and cultural individuation as part of his advocacy of a "Western Islam." In a clear and frequently compelling style, he denounces distortions of a number of Islamic practices among Muslim communities in the West. He calls for a return to a scriptural understanding of Islam, seen as having been deviated from its original message. His writings and lectures have contributed to the emergence of a sense of cultural pride among young women who had developed self-hatred as a result of their social marginalization. In the words of a young woman, "Before I was ashamed of being an Arab."[14] However, Ramadan's ultimate purpose is not to reform conceptions of women but to purify them of their distortions among immigrant Muslim communities in the West. His expository method is worth describing as it sheds light on his tantalizing yet limited ideas about women. He begins by listing the problems encountered by young women in their (immigrant) families, including hastily arranged marriages, denials of divorce, and a sense of victimization, as well as civic disengagement, which he blames on habits acquired in the "countries of emigration." He proceeds to identity problems encountered by women in the West outside of the family and extols the rise of "Islamic feminism" as a movement of women's liberation that differs from the "classical model of the 'liberated Western woman.'" It is "another model of a modern, autonomous, Western, and profoundly Muslim woman."

Although a decentering of Western feminism has already been initiated by a number of women in the West, Ramadan extols the newness of "Islamic feminism" as one in which "many women in the West indicate their right to be respected in their faith by wearing the headscarf and giving visible signs of the modesty in which they wish to be approached: but their faithfulness to Islamic rules does not prevent them from having completely Western tastes when it comes to the style and color of their clothing." In this manner, he gives women credit for having initiated a new form of feminism while at the same time he inscribes it in his conception of Western Islam. He warns that "people in the West would do well to respect this other way of freedom." This procedure allows him to evade criticism for directing (or theorizing) the turn to the veil even as he is engaged in a task similar to that of the evangelists who proselytize among Muslim immigrant communities in Europe, especially in France. They too target women as the assumed weakest link in their mission to convert Muslims to Christianity. Pointedly, Ramadan credits "converts" (to Islam) for energizing this presumed feminist movement. He lauds the scriptural character of the movement as expressing an " 'Islamic femininity' [that] should define a certain way of being and feeling oneself—and wanting to remain—a woman before God and among other human beings, spiritually, socially, politically, and culturally—free, autonomous, and engaged, as the Texts require and societies should guarantee."[15] He is helped in his task by his secretary, Siham Andaloussi, who is emerging as a leading figure in the reveiling trend.[16] One of the converts he undoubtedly had in mind is Dr. Abdallah Thomas Milcent, a Strasbourg physician who supports women's turn to the hijab but also exhorts them to adjust to the pressure placed upon them by wearing a sock hat, bandanna, or turban.[17]

An essential element in Ramadan's method is the blurring of the distinction between din and dunia. He argues that for Muslims the principle of the oneness of God, or *tawhid*, is not confined to worship only. It extends to every facet of a person's life. Thus one cannot profess the unicity of God when one prays on Friday and acts like a heathen on Saturday. The principle of tawhid expresses the need to integrate all the pieces of one's life into a coherent, ethical system of action. Ramadan's perspective resonates with current concerns for wholeness in one's existence, which is constantly threatened by the fragmentation inherent in modern, fast-paced life and the specialized division of labor in industrial societies. However, Ramadan's argument founders on the role he assigns women in a life constructed around tawhid by failing to appreciate their need for wholeness outside of the hijab, which he advocates. He is unconcerned about what it might feel like for a woman to go about her activities with her head tightly wrapped in a headscarf and her corporeal self under pressure of concealment. Neither does he fathom the possibility that ensconcing a woman's body in a special garment might be in effect a discrepant, if not dysfunctional, aspect of tawhid. Indeed, the veil separates, morally and spatially, the Muslim community rather than integrating it as tawhid implies.

Ramadan's conception of tawhid leaves unaddressed women's human need for recognition and social acceptance of their bodies, an integral part of their selves. Barring recognition of this need, Ramadan's emphasis on tawhid as the condition of possibility of Western Muslims' participation in and contribution to their societies is incomplete and one-sided. Ramadan does not ask whether, in convincing a woman of the necessity of the hijab in the context of tawhid, he does not in effect reduce his much touted "need for Him" (God) to a mundane piece of cloth. What a woman is told is that to be whole as a Muslim she must convince herself that she is blemished as a person. Implicitly, she accedes to an ethical life only if she transcends her body by veiling it. From this perspective the female passenger on that hot July day should not have tried to open the window for some air. She should have accepted the heat trapped under her veil as a sort of punishment for being born female. Thus the veil is transformed into a means for atonement.

Ramadan's influence on young French Muslims cannot be ignored. Saïda, the French woman who took up the hijab, points out that "he reassured a whole generation of young people eager to live their lives fully as Muslims in their country but had no clue how to go about it." By writing in French and clearly addressing a European audience, he gave people like Saïda the conviction that they were "thinking Islam in French."[18] Yet this ostensibly new version of religion is indistinguishable from the old (which Saïda rejects as "foreign" because it is elaborated in countries of emigration) even though Saïda, like so many young women in France, thinks the old version is passé.

Claims that the veil symbolizes a new identity notwithstanding, it is inconceivable that Hassiba Boulmelqa, the Algerian sprinter, would have brought her country its first gold medal in 1992 had she trained with a layered headscarf on her head and baggy pants on her legs. Yet some religious critics took her as an example of what was wrong with Algeria: allowing its women to train on tracks, wearing shorts. No one seemed to notice that these critics were in violation of the rule of modesty by gazing at Hassiba in shorts. They were supposed to lower their gaze. They did not give Hassiba her due; they did not congratulate her for putting their country on the Olympic map. The veil was more important in their eyes than her achievement. They did not and could not hail her for having demonstrated to them that a female body can be used for a purpose other than sex. Neither did the critics ponder the implications of Hassiba's success: there were numerous other women who could have plied their bodies for similar achievement but were concealing them instead so as not to offend the critics' conception of gender decorum.

The West as an outer limit to women's corporeal self is best illustrated by critiques of the Western women's movement developed by male and female veil advocates: "Feminism is an unnatural, artificial and abnormal product of modern day disintegration which in turn is the inevitable result of the rejection of all moral and spiritual values."[19] Furthermore,

> The question of absolute equality between man and woman is a complete nonsense according to Islam. . . . Islam confers equal rights on the women and men in various fields of life. As a human being woman enjoys equal status and equal rights with man. But in certain spheres of life, Islam makes distinctions between a man and a woman and bestows different rights and obligations on them. It is not on account of any hatred or prejudice against any sex but due to the natural, biological differences between the sexes. Islam has taken these differences into account and has assigned distinct roles and functions to each sex.[20]

Implicitly, this criticism of feminism conflates a woman's call for improvement of her status in society with rejection of Islam and adoption of non-Muslim values. The point is well illustrated by a female fundamentalist: "These limits [the veil, avoidance of grooming, and confinement to one's home] are in opposition to those who call for giving the woman what they consider complete freedom. . . . Is going to work and to toil by women, mixing with men outside the house, and abandoning her home and children freeing her?"[21] The male advocate of veiling quoted above describes women's presumed domestic vocation in no uncertain terms: "Imagine for a while the plight of a land or naval force which wholly consists of women. It is quite possible that right in the midst of war, a fair number of them might be down with menstrual discharge, a good number of delivery cases forced to stay in bed, and a fair percentage of pregnant ones fuming and skulking uselessly. One may say that the military service is rather too strenuous for women."[22] The flight of fancy that this statement reflects is all the more remarkable in that it was written after the Abu Ghraib scandal in Iraq revealed that American women soldiers were involved in the sexual torture of men (and women) not only in Iraq but also at Guantanamo Bay.[23] However, whenever convenient, Western knowledge is harnessed as proof that women should not mingle with men or work outside their homes.[24]

Imagining the West as a corruptor of women overshadows the far more threatening role that the West plays as an enabler and defender of conservative politics in the Middle East. Women are unfairly made to atone for the West's imperial history. The focus on the veil as a marker of the divide between East and West, Islam and Christianity, faith and faithlessness, obscures this basic fact that women have little to do with the sociopolitical dynamics that encourage men to retreat into a dysfunctional custom to protect *their* sense of self and identity. No country in the Muslim world would be in danger of cultural extinction if all women were to jettison the veil. But it would mean that male advocates of veiling would have to make adjustments to their perception of themselves. They would have to understand that they are no less men for accepting women as their social equals—for accepting that a woman's body is hers to live, not a man's prerogative to regulate in its most minute details of grooming, dressing, and (most important) experiencing. Conversely, a woman would have to ask herself why she looks on as a man arrogates to himself the right to advocate for the veil, speak in the name of God, and use persuasion or coercion to keep a woman in line with *his* conception of *her* body.

I suspect that coming to terms with women, accepting their humanness, also means that a man must accept himself as a fallible human being, one among many, who cannot demand any power of oversight over how a woman should dress or groom her body. A man's absorption in the details of a woman's relation to her body is an assault on her dignity. It also violates her freedom of conscience, as her body and mind affect each other. We oppose brainwashing as a violation of conscience, so why can we not oppose the straightjacketing of a woman's body in a myriad of rules that specify whether a woman should pluck her eyebrows, wear stiletto heels, or visit the grave of a loved one?[25] Such rules are a constant reminder that a woman's body does not belong to her, and by implication she does not belong to herself. This is hardly conducive to a woman's sense of autonomy.

The West is thus a constant referent for veiling advocates. Its enduring role in women's and men's imaginary needs to be demystified. It is one thing to oppose Western prejudices against Islam and Western incursions in Muslim countries; it is another to conflate women's capacity to seek respect and bodily autonomy with men's incapacity to change their worldviews or create viable political and economic institutions. In fact, the reveiling trend deflects attention from problems such as the feminization of poverty or elusive political rights onto a resymbolization of the veil. To think that veiling oneself constructively assuages anger at the West is illusory. Besides, there are women and men in the West who are equally angry at their government's involvement in unjust wars in the Middle East. Returning to the veil means stepping back into a past that was not always beneficial to women. It takes greater courage and foresight to assert a full measure of one's humanity by resisting the pressure (no matter its origin) to take up the veil. Identity politics that rests on a headscarf and a dress leads nowhere but to a renewed focus on the body as a "natural" limitation of a woman's life. Watching over how much of a woman's flesh shows through a dress can hardly stimulate reflection on how to move Muslim societies toward a better future, or how to end anti-Muslim prejudice. Similarly, making a little girl wear a mini hijab is hardly conducive to elevating her sights above her headscarf.

The current reveiling trend is not a sign of greater piety or infusion of religious morality in a world that has admittedly lost its moral compass. In Algeria, groups that coerced women into wearing veils in the 1990s also engaged in acts of violence against them for working as hairdressers or practicing divination arts. Some women were also forced into "temporary marriage" (*mut'a*), a Shi'i Islam custom that is alien to Algeria and essentially meant raping women with impunity.[26] Clearly not all the parties engaged in a war against the Algerian state condoned this practice. Nevertheless, by focusing on women as embodiments of the ills of "Western" culture, they set the tone for the mistreatment of women. No warring group (including the state army or police) issued a statement condemning the practice or recommending that women be left out of the battle raging between men. The ongoing war in Iraq caused upward of three million people to seek refuge in neighboring countries, especially Syria and Jordan. Women report that prostitution has become rife among refugees, often supervised by impoverished male relatives. The Iraqi government seems unconcerned with the plight of women, just as it has kept silent over the abuse of women in detention centers and stood by while tribal customs inimical to women have been revived and violence against women is on the rise. This means that the groups and institutions that preside over veiling are also the ones that have little respect for women's dignity and right to be. Consequently, women need to disengage from the Westing of the West by making out what is good for them as human beings. When they know that veiling shapes their perception of themselves or have doubts about its effect on them, they should not wear a veil. Not wearing a veil is no more a byproduct of the West than eating wheat imported from the United States makes one American.

Moving Forward

In these letters I cast doubt on the validity of the arguments usually invoked by women who take up the hijab. I have shown that modesty is neither secured nor enhanced by the veil. If chastity is the flip side of modesty, the veil is no guarantee for it either; it lies instead with a woman's conscious decision to manage her sexuality according to her conception of herself in awareness of the social forces (whether religious or more mundane) that seek to wrest from her the moral autonomy necessary for her to make that decision. Similarly, the veil is no protection from sexual harassment. In reality, it may even stimulate more harassment as a number of men are not sure that a woman is not wearing a veil because she is seeking greater freedom from her family rather than out of religious conviction. Besides, men themselves may be ambivalent about the religious status of the veil; they may not see it as an impediment to making sexual advances to a woman or even committing rape. For example, a veiled Saudi woman was raped as she was sitting in a car with a former boyfriend.[27]

Nevertheless, the reveiling trend acutely poses the question of a woman's agency, her freedom to choose. Many of the women who have taken up the veil have argued that they did so willingly either as a deliberate decision to display pride in their culture or out of religious conviction. I have explained that there is no compelling reason to make the veil the sole sign of pride in one's culture. The selection of the veil as *the* symbolic representation of Islamic culture is reductive as well as ideological. It reduces a complex culture to a contested custom and embeds women's "choice" in a narrative of advocacy for the veil that transcends the goal of achieving cultural pride. Conviction as a motivation for donning the veil is unimpeachable when it stems from a personal reflection on metaphysical issues untrammeled by political, ideological, and economic considerations. Yet, like the other justifications of veiling, conviction does not escape the overdetermining power of the context within which it occurs, which shapes its contours as well as its timing. Context is the most important factor that undermines the validity as well as the legitimacy of justifications for the veil at the current historical conjuncture.

A woman veiling herself in Paris is making a statement about her place in French society that has refused to treat her as a full-fledged citizen; it perceives her as "allogenic" and permanently marked as an "immigrant" no matter the depth of her French roots.[28] The veil for this woman signifies the appropriation of a sign that has been so politicized as to mean the rejection of French society. To the use of French culture as a weapon with which she was bludgeoned, this woman uses an equally powerful cultural weapon to defend herself. By the same token, she finds comfort in acknowledging and assuming her Islamic heritage, which she may have repressed for the sake of assimilation into the dominant value system of her society. She revels in her new visibility as a wearer of a reviled custom.

A woman veiling herself in New York also makes a statement about the positivity of her culture in a social climate strained by the Iraq and Afghan wars. Like her Paris counterpart, she too revels in her new visibility. Meanwhile, in Istanbul a woman is fighting her own (culturally Muslim) government for the *right* to wear a veil and put an end to a ban on headscarves. She is a native Turk contesting the intrusive power of the state in her personal life. However, no matter how legitimate these women's goals are, the choice of the veil as an instrument for fighting prejudice is vitiated for a number of reasons: Historically, the veil is a custom common to most women throughout the Muslim world. When a woman takes it up in one country as a major aspect of her Islamicity, she validates its use for women in another country who may find it difficult to argue against it. In this sense, a woman's "choice" of the veil engages her responsibility toward other women. The fight for recognition of the veil as summing up Islam that takes place in Paris, New York, or Istanbul necessarily affects the women in Riyadh and Tehran who are compelled by law to wear it. As a custom grounded in history and sanctified by theologians, the veil is never innocent; it is not what it seems to be—a mark of religiosity. It is part of a historic power configuration in which men, with or without religious fervor, have found sustenance for their identity as males. It is difficult to extirpate the veil from the thick history of men's power. In Algeria during the colonial era, many a brother took a veiled woman as a stand-in for a sister or a mother whose property he coveted and made his. It is also power that a man defends when he advocates for the veil or imposes it on a fiancée as the sine qua non for marrying her.

However, the temptation of the veil is as real as it is misleading. The veil has been tantalizing to Muslims and non-Muslims, including intellectuals. Attempts to present it as a tool of empowerment of women rest on a dubious postmodernist conception of power according to which whatever a woman undertakes to do is liberating as long as she thinks that she is engaged in some form of "resistance" or self-assertion, no matter how misguided.[29] Moreover, the veil has been hailed as part of a process of demystification of modernity insofar as it represents a woman's engagement in action she deems correct rather than her believing in correct ideas.[30] This rationalization disembeds the veil from the history that gave it birth and reinserts it as a new factor in the complex dynamics of the present.[31] Furthermore, non-Muslim women who have taken up the study of veiling compound the reification of the veil and provide more mystifications of veiling in the name of social science research. But unless these women are prepared to don the veil themselves, they should realize the implications of imparting to it meanings that reinforce its rehabilitation as a custom that reduces women to their biological body and denies them autonomy *in* their body. Cultural relativism should not obscure the real effects of veiling on a woman's psyche as she lives out her concrete existence. Nor should it make palatable the massive and essentialist conception of gender difference that the veil embodies, for this would mean agreeing that the veil is divinely ordained—a sacralization task that eludes sanction from social science.

The veil, no matter what style (face-baring or face-covering), is hardly an answer to the search for alternative ways to enter or negotiate the intricacies of a postmodern world. Some styles of veiling are made to obliterate women's existence in public space and can hardly foster in a woman a sense of her presence in the world. Each woman is thus made to carry a symbolic monastery on her back that oddly makes her obliteration visible to others. No one is entitled to flaunt the merits of veiling without considering the damage that they do to the multitude of women who, Muslim in their hearts, nevertheless refuse to validate the monopoly over faith seized by self-styled censors of morality.

Intellectualizing the veil can lead to attractive theories about modernity (reduced to mean Western women's dress, women mixing with men, or work), secularism, and civilization "clashes," all of which serve to legitimize the veil in one way or another. The veil is hardly an instrument with which to claim a new form of modernity or resist modernity. Advocates of veiling could not care less for what we call modernity. They do not come from another planet; they were born to a world that has seen fetishes of modernity in many forms—as a cassette player, a television set with satellite dish, a car, or the more ubiquitous cell phone, among others. However, their defense of the veil is a defense of the sphere of their intimacy. And this has traditionally been defended from and against women prior to the onset of the discourse on modernity. As a man whose daughters—all of whom are accomplished career women—do not wear the veil, but whose wife had to wear one, recently said to me, "I am the one in command" (in his home). And being in command is what the veil is about. Besides, the veil, even when assumed willingly, is not synonymous with action, modern, postmodern, or hypermodern. At the risk of belaboring the point, the veil is not action, it is reaction; it is repetition of the past.

Islam is not reducible to the veil, and the veil does not sum up religion. There is nothing elevating about the veil spiritually or politically. But it is the last refuge of men's (sexual) identity. If Western men have found different ways of protecting their identity than by insisting on chastity belts or laws against adultery, it is because they were compelled to by the unrelenting efforts of women advocating for their right to self-determination in body, mind, and action. This in no way means that these men no longer feel superior to women. It means that they express their superiority in different ways from the past, and where they do it in violation of the law (as in sexual harassment) they sometimes get punished for it. It also means that their identity is in a constant state of destabilization.

If the veil does not in and of itself provide an alternative to life in a "modern" society, it lends itself to symbolic meanings and countermeanings; it is entangled in multiple layers of meaning. When a woman wears it, she garbles its meanings insofar as she never knows which one of these will be perceived by others as the one she has attributed to it. Ironically, as a woman thinks that she is making a clear statement by wearing a veil, she loses control over its meaning. Yet she assumes all of the meanings that have been historically associated with it. In other words, there is no way in which the veil can be rehabilitated and made to represent something different from what it has been. It is not a tool that can be reshaped and made to serve a different purpose. The veil is its purpose. It has no depth but is woven with multiple strands of meanings. Modesty, chastity, protection from sexual harassment, and conviction combine to obscure the purpose of the veil: the empowerment of a man over a woman in the intimacy of their sexual identity as borne by their bodies.

In the past, in writing about women's involvement in the Algerian war of decolonization (1954–62), I pointed out that they had acted as people who had suffered from colonial rule, as members of a society that had been subjected to grave injustice. I took issue with those who dismissed women's engagement as misguided and naïve because it was incommensurate with the gains received in the aftermath of the independence of Algeria.[32] I stand by what I wrote, and I do not think that the women who veil themselves today in Algiers, Paris, or New York are engaged in the same struggle as Algerian women were in the 1950s, when they freed themselves of the veil *in order* to make history.

The war in Iraq bears similarities to the Algerian war in military strategy and the logic of conquest. It has been a setback for women, whose condition has been aggravated. However, a reveiling trend had started under Saddam Hussein's rule, albeit as a reflection of deteriorating socioeconomic conditions due to twelve years of embargo subsequent to the first Gulf War and ten years of war against Iran. Similarly, Afghan women had been caught in the midst of a long civil war that brought to the fore the Taliban, and they continue to be the casualties of ongoing battles between U.S./NATO troops and local warlords. They were forced not only to wear the burqa but also to refrain from working, among other restrictions. Given these circumstances, it is difficult to see how the veil could be perceived as a tool of liberation or a symbol of resistance for women who wear it outside of these war zones. These women are not taking up the veil in solidarity with Iraqi or Afghan women. That would be pure absurdity. Interestingly, a woman advocate of Al Qaeda's worldview and wearer of the veil that leaves only slits for the eyes (the niqab) nevertheless found it intolerable to don the burqa as required when she visited Afghanistan; she asked permission to wear a different style.[33] Choosing between veils or swapping one veil for another may provide the illusion of choice, but in reality it leaves women hampered by their bodies instead of living them. In despair an occasional woman prefers to immolate herself rather than be forced to wear a veil, as did the Iranian physician Homa Darabi in 1994; she had been unable to leave her country because her husband refused to give his consent.

It is often said that Middle East societies have not had a renaissance, although past achievements of Muslim civilization contributed to the West's. Can the veil be seen as an attempt at rejuvenating Muslim civilization? The answer is a resounding no. Not wearing the veil is not a victory of the "West," it is women's victory over a custom that inflects their thinking about themselves as *human* beings. Wearing the veil is not a strike against anti-Muslim prejudice. It is a strike against women's capacity to distinguish between freedom and autonomy of conscience and uncritical acceptance of morally degrading regulations of their bodies. Wearing the veil is not the triumph of Islam over its detractors. At the present historical conjuncture, it degrades Islam to the level of a creed and impoverishes its humanistic import.[34] This is the time for women to free themselves of it and by the same token free men, too. Whether they live in the "West" or in Muslim societies, women are faced with the task of teasing out passing trends and fads from long-term change. Present times challenge all of us in our most intimate thoughts and feelings, in our minds and hearts, in our dignity and sense of outrage.

As long as states mandate or prohibit veiling, as long as political movements advocate for it, as long as organized networks with books, lectures, DVDs, and course packets promote it far and wide, a woman can never be sure that she takes up a veil freely, in full awareness of its meanings and effects. Ultimately, there is no compelling justification for veiling, not even faith. For it, too, needs to confront the power nexus that sustains the repetition of the *history* of the veil. No one is entitled to turn the veil into a political flag, and no one should derive satisfaction from its removal except women themselves.

Notes

INTRODUCTION

1. Both constitutions contain a provision upholding the primacy of "rules of Islam" over any contravening law. See my "Women: The Trojan Horse of Islam and Geopolitics," in *Islam and the Orientalist World System*, ed. Mazhar Al Zo'by and Khaldoun Samman (London: Enigma Books, 2008), 55–76.

2. Quoted in Marcel Bisiaux and Catherine Jajolet, *A ma mère: 50 écrivains parlent de leur mère* (Paris: Pierre Horay, 1988–2006), 310.

3. BBC News, "Saudi Police 'Stopped' Fire Rescue," March 15, 2002, http://news.bbc.co.uk/2/hi/middle_east/1874471.stm (accessed May 21, 2008). The religious police are referred to as the Commission for the Promotion of Virtue and Prevention of Vice.

4. See, among others, Arlene Elowe MacLeod, *Accommodating Protest: Working Women, the New Veil and Change in Cairo* (New York: Columbia University Press, 1991); Katherine Bullock, *Rethinking Muslim Women and the Veil: Challenging Historical and Modern Stereotypes* (Herndon, VA: International Institute of Islamic Thought, 2003); Leila Hessini, "Wearing the Hijab in Contemporary Morocco: Choice and Identity," in *Reconstructing*

Gender in the Middle East: Tradition, Identity and Power, ed. Fatma Müge Göçek and Shiva Balaghi (New York: Columbia University Press, 1994), 40–56; Homa Hoodfar, "Return to the Veil: Personal Strategies and Public Participation in Egypt," in *Working Women: International Perspectives on Labor and Gender Ideology*, ed. Nanneke Redclift and M. Thea Sinclair (London: Routledge, 1991), 104–24. Hoodfar specifically claims that she gives women a voice (see p. 105). In a similar vein, a 1982 documentary film, *A Veiled Revolution*, directed by Marilyn Gaunt and produced by Elizabeth Fernea, presented reveiling as a "revolution."

5. Where a researcher acknowledges the "unveiled" women's perspectives as necessary to include in her analysis, she describes these as representing a "war" that pits their proponents against veiled women. See Sherifa Zuhur, *Revealing Reveiling: Islamist Ideology in Contemporary Egypt* (Albany: State University of New York, 1992), 133.

6. Yet veiling existed in non-Muslim societies such as ancient Greece and early Judaic and Christian societies. If veiling had been studied in these societies as it is today in the Muslim world, we would be intrigued by the lack of rigor, the theoretical dubiousness, and the ahistorical methods used by researchers.

7. Interviews I carried out in Istanbul in 1999 revealed that some faculty members objected to acting as implementing agents of a state policy they felt was discriminatory.

8. Sabrina Tavernese, "Turkey's High Court Overturns Headscarf Rule," *New York Times*, June 6, 2008.

9. Gisèle Halimi, "Laïcité: Une loi pour la cohésion, 23 Octobre 2003," 2, http://sisyphe.org/article.php3?id_article=730 (accessed December 11, 2007).

10. Quoted in Ajay Singh Chaudhary, "'The Simulacra of Morality': Islamic Veiling, Religious Politics and the Limits of Liberalism," *Dialectical Anthropology* 29 (2005): 364.

11. In addition to MacLeod, *Accommodating Protest*, see, for example, Nilüfer Göler, *The Forbidden Modern: Civilization and Veiling* (Ann Arbor: University of Michigan Press, 1996); and Susan Brenner, "Reconstructing Self and Society: Javanese Muslim Women," *American Ethnologist* 23, 4 (1996): 673–97. Brenner argues that veiling ushers in a new form of modernity. Also see

Pat Mule and Diane Barthel "The Return to the Veil: Individual Autonomy vs. Social Esteem, *Sociological Forum* 7, 2 (June 1994): 323–32. For insight into modernity, gender, and the veil, see Afsaneh Najmabadi, "Veiled Discourse—Unveiled Bodies," *Feminist Studies* 19, 3 (Autumn 1993): 487–518, which contradicts her interpretation of veiling in "Feminism in an Islamic Republic: Years of Hardship, Years of Growth," in *Women and Gender: Social Change in the Muslim World*, ed. Yvonne Y. Haddad and John Esposito (New York: Oxford University Press, 1998), 59–84.

12. The word *hijab* is used in the Quran to refer to the "separation" or "curtain" behind which uninvited guests or callers to Prophet Muhammad's household presumably were enjoined to stand to speak to his wives.

13. The original meaning of the word *jilbab* (a long garment that covers the body) has changed depending on regions. In Indonesia, for instance, jilbab may refer to head cover only. But in recent times it has been used to refer to head cover as well as a long, loose dress, as befits the new veiling trend. It is equivalent to hijab. See Brenner, "Reconstructing Self," 674 and fn. 5; Fadwa El Guindi, *Veil: Modesty, Privacy and Resistance* (Oxford: Berg, 1999), 139. Brenner notes that there was no indigenous veiling that would be comparable to the trend that has taken hold in the past two decades. The type of veiling commonly used in western Algeria, which is gradually disappearing in favor of the hijab, is a white square of cotton or silk that a woman drapes around her body and over her head and face, leaving an aperture for one eye made by folding two corners of the wrap over and keeping them in place with one hand.

14. *Niqab* is sometimes used interchangeably with jilbab. It is a piece of thin cloth, such as muslin, that sits on the bridge of the nose and covers a woman's features except her eyes. A woman may add another piece of black muslin to cover over the eyes. In Algiers, until recently, the niqab was a triangular piece of white muslin (the *'adjar*) with two strings that tie in the back of the head below the large body wrap that also covers the head; it can also be a piece of black muslin cut in such a way as to cover forehead, nose, and mouth but leave slits for the eyes.

15. For a useful discussion of the veil terminology, see El Guindi, *Veil*, 151–57. Generic names for the veil vary from country

to country (*chador* in Iran, *jallaba* in Morocco, *gallabiya* in Egypt, *haik* in Algeria, *burqa* in Afghanistan, purdah in Pakistan, 'abaya in Saudi Arabia, etc.) but coexist with the increasingly transnational term hijab.

LETTER ONE

1. The dictionary gives *sitar* as the noun derived from the verb *satara*. See J. Milton Cowan, ed., *The Hans Wehr Dictionary of Modern Written Arabic* (Ithaca: Spoken Languages Services, 1976).

2. The North African *jallaba* is different in style from the Egyptian *gallabiya* worn by common men, which is a long, shirt-like dress. The *jallaba* is usually woven in wool and worn in cold weather. Its variant for women is longer and cut out of cotton.

3. The *qashabyia* style of veiling is used mostly in western Algeria, although it coexists with the hijab, an import from Egypt.

4. It has been reported that a Strasbourg high school student of Turkish descent, Cennet Dogayan, shaved her head in response to the March 25, 2004, law forbidding the headscarf in French public schools. See http://www.oumma.com/le-film-Un-racisme-à-peine-voilé (accessed December 11, 2007).

5. See introduction, notes 13 and 14.

6. According to the *Hans Wehr Dictionary of Modern Written Arabic*, *khimar* derives from the verb *khamara*, which means to hide, conceal, or cover. Translators of the Quran use their knowledge of the custom of veiling to read it back into the original text and thus fail to capture the nuances of meaning of words such as *khimar*. The khimar today is a fitted garment that slips over the head and falls over the shoulders and the bosom. In some instances it covers the hips. See also the discussion of the jilbab in the introduction.

7. Sura 24:31, *The Glorious Qur'an*, text and explanatory trans. Muhammad Marmaduke Pickthall (Islamic Call Society: Socialist People's Arab Jamahiriya, n.d.). I am using this old translation because it denotes the translator's desire to be "modest" in translating the word *furuj*, or pudenda, and represents a standard rendition of the original. Contemporary male advocates of veiling also use "modesty" in the translation of this sura. See Muhammad

Sharif Chaudhry, *Women's Rights in Islam* (New Delhi: Adam, 2008), 98. Ahmed Ali translates *furuj* as "private parts." See *Al-Qur'an: A Contemporary Translation*, by Ahmed Ali (Princeton: Princeton University Press, 1993).

8. *Al-Qur'an*, trans. Ali.

9. The Arabic root of *zina* is *zin*, which means beauty. *Zina* refers to enhancement of beauty.

10. *Le Coran: Essai de traduction*, revised and corrected ed. (Paris: Albin Michel, 1995), 375.

11. Sura 24:30 reads: "Tell the believing men to lower their gaze and be modest. That is purer for them. Lo! Allah is Aware of what they do." *The Glorious Quran*, trans. Pickthall. As with the sura focusing on women, Ali translates *furuj* as "private parts."

12. Anwar Moazzam, *Jamal al-Din al-Afghani: A Muslim Intellectual* (New Delhi: Concept, 1984), 78.

13. See G. F. Schueler, "Why Modesty Is a Virtue," *Ethics* 107, 3 (April 1997): 467–85. See also a response to Schueler by Julia Driver, "Modesty and Ignorance," *Ethics* 109, 4 (July 1999): 827–34.

14. Richard T. Antoun, "On the Modesty of Women in Arab Muslim Villages: A Study in the Accommodation of Traditions," *American Anthropologist*, new series 70, 4 (August 1968): 672–73.

15. Upon reading this letter, a doctor of theology questioned the distinction I made between din and dunia; he argued that "the authentic message of Islam [is] the reconstruction of dunia by din. Since the creator of dunia is Allah, he has an authority to establish *dunia*." The first part of the argument is theologically correct, but it does not make allowance for the difference between what is ideal/normative and what is existential.

16. Patrick Michel suggests the intriguing idea that religion may not be an identity in itself, although its uses as such may reflect an "identity problem," which could not be expressed without it. See his "Espace ouvert, identités plurielles: les recompositions contemporaines du croire," *Social Compass* 53, 2 (2006): 237.

17. My use of the concept of stigma is different from Nilüfer Göler's as expressed in her "Voluntary Adoption of Islamic Stigma Symbols," *Social Research* 70, 3 (Fall 2003).

18. Al-Afghani listed *haya'*, shame, as one of the "three qualities produced by religion," in addition to trustworthiness and

truthfulness. Nikki R. Keddie, *An Islamic Response to Imperialism: Political and Religious Writings of Sayyid Jamal ad-Din "al Afghani"* (Berkeley: University of California Press, 1968), 144–47.

19. A staff member of an Islamic institution in New York City mentioned to me in the course of a discussion on veiling that common women "do not know why they wear the veil." This dismissal of poor women's acceptance of a custom that has traditionally been enforced by men was jarring.

20. See Elaine Sciolino and Souad Mekhennet, "Muslim Women and Virginity: 2 Worlds Collide," *New York Times*, June 11, 2008.

21. See sura 24:30 quoted in note 11 above.

22. Legal scholars belonging to the Maliki and Hanbali schools of law allow for a woman's face and hands to be free, especially when she is giving testimony, is on trial, and is "in marriage." See Qasim Amin, *The Liberation of Women and the New Woman*, trans. Samiha Sidhom Peterson (Cairo: American University in Cairo Press, 2004), 38–39.

23. Lila Abu-Lughod describes the public "repentance" of female actresses in Egypt in the 1990s who took up the hijab and either retired or continued acting in a hijab. These women's turn to the veil was aided by male religious figures. See *Dramas of Nationhood: The Politics of Television in Egypt* (Chicago: University of Chicago Press, 2005), 243–45.

24. See Leïla Djitli, *Lettre à ma fille qui veut porter le voile* (Lonrai, Normandie: Doc en Stock/Editions de la Martinière, 2004). This is an imaginative story written by a journalist familiar with life in the Paris ghettos.

25. In real life, Katherine Bullock reports that the three-year-old son of one of her veiled respondents wished to understand why Muslim men do not wear veils like women do. He was told that it is because they "do not want the men to see ummi [Mum] because women are beautiful." The explanation begs the question as to why beauty must be covered. See *Rethinking Muslim Women*, 71.

26. See Connie Koppelman, "The Politics of Hair," *Frontiers: A Journal of Women's Studies* 17, 2 (1996): 87–88.

27. St. Paul grounded his injunction in the prevailing understanding of God being the head of Christ, the latter the head of

man, and man the head of woman. While man is the "glory" of God, woman is the glory of man. Discussions of 1 Cor. 11:10 are insightful because they shed light on the relationship between religion and social custom, as well between man and woman, about who has authority on a woman's "head," literally and figuratively. See M. D. Hooker, "Authority on Her Head: An Examination of I COR. XI.10," *New Testament Studies* 10 (October 1963): 410–16; and Annie Jaubert, "Le voile des femmes (I COR. XI.2–16)," *New Testament Studies* 18 (October 1972): 419–30.

28. These are meanings of the verb *baraja*, from which *mutabarrajat* is derived.

29. Sura 24:60, trans. Ahmed Ali. In his translation, Muhammad Sharif Chaudhry inserts the word "modesty" in lieu of "avoid" in a clear attempt to discount the context of the sura. He wrote, "but it is best for them to be modest." See his *Women's Rights in Islam*, 99. Others added "women past child bearing age" before "who have no hope of marriage."

30. *Thaub* in some cultures is used only in the context of the clothing the pilgrims to Mecca must wear during the pilgrimage ritual. It is noteworthy, however, that the dictionary gives "mask" as a figurative meaning of this word.

31. Amin, *The Liberation of Women*, 156–57.

32. Islamists active in poor urban neighborhoods entice women into wearing the hijab by offering it to them free of charge. Some of Zuhur's respondents reported that a number of women had been paid by the Egyptian Muslim Brothers to wear the hijab and refrain from working outside their home. See her *Revealing Reveiling*, 77.

LETTER TWO

1. *Al-Qur'an*, trans. Ali.

2. Chaudhry, *Women's Rights in Islam*, 99.

3. Amin, *The Liberation of Women*, 54.

4. *The Non-Muslim Hijabi: Niqab Using Shayla Scarf*, http://youtube.com/watch?v=Z7JycC8X9e4; *The Non-Muslim Hijabi: The Earring Edition*, http://youtube.com/watch?v=sICPLzBbU IU&feature=related; *The Non-Muslim Hijabi: Thoughts on Hijab*,

http://youtube.com/watch?v=xel1o-o6I5g&feature=related (accessed May 9, 2008).

LETTER THREE

1. Djitli, *Lettre à ma fille*, 8.

2. For example, she supports the rights of lesbian, gay, bisexual, and queer people (LGBQ), which would be unlikely for a woman who dons the hijab for religious reasons.

3. The March 15, 2004, law prohibits wearing "symbols of clothing by which students conspicuously manifest a religious appearance." Such signs also include the Christian cross and the Jewish yarmulke. Students who refused to comply with the headdress ban were expelled.

4. Wahabism is the religious doctrine prevalent in Saudi Arabia. It was formulated in the eighteenth century by Muhammad Ibn Abd al Wahab and promotes an extremely restrictive view of women and their role in society, among others.

5. Sabrina Tavernise, "Under a Scarf, a Turkish Lawyer Fighting to Wear It," *New York Times*, February 9, 2008.

6. See, among others, http://www.LibertyPost.org (accessed June 15, 2008).

LETTER FOUR

1. AMAL is the acronym of the Shi'i militia, Afwaj al-Muqawwama Al-Lubnaniyya, translated as the Lebanese Resistance Detachments, that advocates for the rights of the Shi'i population and played a significant role during the Lebanese civil war before merging with Hezbollah in 1983.

2. Amina Wadud, *Inside the Gender Jihad: Women's Reform in Islam* (Oxford: One World Publishers, 2006), 223.

3. Ibid., 177.

4. Ibid., 221.

5. Anissa's case is different from those studied in Egypt and Morocco. She did not use the hijab in order to continue to work. See introduction, note 4.

6. I have critically analyzed her views in my "Consequences of Political Liberalization and Socio-Cultural Mobilization for Women in Algeria, Egypt and Jordan," in *Governing Women: Women's Political Effectiveness in Contexts of Democratization and Governance Reform*, ed. Anne-Marie Goetz (New York: Routledge, 2009), 45–62.

7. See Saba Mahmood, *Politics of Piety: The Islamic Revival and the Feminist Subject* (Princeton: Princeton University Press, 2005).

8. Azza Karam, *Women, Islamisms and the State: Contemporary Feminisms in Egypt* (New York: St. Martin's, 1998).

9. The Al Maghrib Institute was formed in 2001 by young imams in the United States and Canada. In addition to a bachelor's degree in Islamic sciences, it provides speakers to groups seeking to increase their knowledge of Islam. Its website claims that it has the largest Islamic sciences student body in North America, with three thousand students. See http://www.almaghrib.org.

10. Ghulam Sarwar, *Islam: Beliefs and Teachings*, rev. ed. (New Delhi: Markazi Maktaba Islami Publishers, 2000), 168.

11. Ibid., 169–70.

12. Ibid., 145.

13. See letter 2, note 4, for the relevant URLs.

14. In Islam, *tawhid* is an established principle that affirms the indivisibility and oneness of God, which by implication requires worship undifferentiated by gender.

15. Quoted in Dounia Bouzar and Saïda Kada, *L'une voilée, l'autre pas* (Paris: Albin Michel, 2003), 22.

16. See Göler, *The Forbidden Modern*, 103.

17. Wearing a black veil is not a universally accepted style. In Algeria, for example, the prevailing style of veiling prior to the reveiling trend was white, except in the eastern city of Constantine, where it is black.

18. Bouzar and Kada, *L'une voilée*, 34.

19. Göler, *The Forbidden Modern*, 104–5.

20. See Amel Boubekeur, "Modernité des jeunes filles voilées," *CERAS Projet, Recherches et Actions Sociales*, no. 287 (July 2005), http://www.ceras-projet.com/index.php?id=1134 (accessed November 11, 2007). It must be noted that dating between young

veiled women and men has occurred in Algeria for quite some time, albeit receiving little attention from analysts.

21. For a discussion of the legal implications of the veil, see Nusrat Choudhury, "From the Stasi Commission to the European Court of Human Rights: *L'Affaire du Foulard* and the Challenge of Protecting the Rights of Muslim Girls," *Columbia Journal of Gender and Law* 16 (January 2007): 199–290.

22. Quoted in Bouzar and Kada, *L'une voilée*, 50–51.

23. The role of other imams in the French suburban ghettoes was studied by Dounia Bouzar, *L'Islam des banlieues, les prédicateurs musulmans, nouveaux travailleurs sociaux?* (Paris: Syros-La Découverte, 2001).

24. It is interesting to note that second-generation male immigrants in France have become aware that the instrumental use of Muslim identity (expressed as a reflexive rejection of the prevailing culture) was self-defeating because they found out that they had defended a predefined Muslim and oppositional identity they had not taken the time to understand. See Bouzar and Kada, *L'une voilée*, 124.

LETTER FIVE

1. See, among others, Marnia Lazreg, *Torture and the Twilight of Empire: From Algiers to Baghdad* (Princeton: Princeton University Press, 2008), chap. 6.

2. Faegheh Shirazi, *The Veil Unveiled: The Hijab in Modern Culture* (Gainesville: University Press of Florida, 2001), 105.

3. Ibid., 133.

4. Asma Barlas argues that the Quran refers to the use of the veil (the jilbab) to protect women from *jahili* (men who had not at the time converted to Islam), not from Muslim men who were enjoined to be as sexually modest as women. See *Believing Women in Islam: Unreading Patriarchal Interpretations of the Qur'an* (Austin: University of Texas Press, 2002), 50–58.

5. Quoted in Moazzam, *Jamal al-Din al-Afghani*, 64. On al-Afghani, see also Keddie, *An Islamic Response to Imperialism*.

6. Amin, *The Liberation of Women*, 37. For a feminist critique of Amin, see, among others, Lila Abu-Lughod, "The Marriage

of Feminism and Islamism in Egypt: Selective Repudiation as a Dynamic of Postcolonial Cultural Politics," in *Remaking Women: Feminism and Modernity in the Middle East*, ed. Lila Abu-Lughod (Princeton: Princeton University Press, 1998), 258–61.

7. Ibid., 35. Ambivalence about the religious status of the veil resurfaced among Muslim leaders asked by the French government to express their opinion on the draft law of *laïcité* (secularity) that was passed on March 15, 2004. Opinions ran the gamut from suggesting that in the Quran veiling is a mere recommendation to women and not an obligation, to viewing it as a secondary and negotiable obligation, to declaring it an integral part of dogma. See Frank Fregosi, "Champs religieux official et contre-champ islamique," in *La politisation du voile en France, en Europe et dans le monde arabe*, ed. Françoise Lorcerie (Paris: L'Harmattan, 2005), 58–63. Such opinions reflected not only the influence of the country of origin of the leaders (Algeria, Morocco, Turkey, and the Gulf states) but also their relation to the role of Islam in geopolitics.

8. Ibid., 48.

9. See Boubekeur, "Modernité des jeunes filles voilées."

10. See Joan Scott, *The Politics of the Veil* (Princeton: Princeton University Press, 2007), chap. 5.

11. Shirazi, *The Veil Unveiled*, 98–105.

12. For example, raising women's status through education, more equitable laws regulating divorce and polygyny, and putting an end to veiling the face and "seclusion" were Qasim Amin's goals.

13. Marnia Lazreg, *The Eloquence of Silence: Algerian Women in Question* (New York: Routledge, 1994), 217.

14. Bouzar and Kada, *L'une voilée*, 89.

15. Tariq Ramadan, *Western Muslims and the Future of Islam* (Oxford: Oxford University Press, 2004), 140, 142, 143. His work acquires greater significance as providing an alternative to women in the context of France, where some women's associations are actively engaged in "training" young women from immigrant families in methods of standing up to their parents.

16. See Amel Boubekeur, "Female Religious Professionals in France," *ISIM Newsletter*, no. 14 (June 2004): 28. ISIM is the acronym for the International Institute for the Study of Islam in the Modern World.

17. Abdallah Thomas Milcent, "Rentrée 2004. Mode d'emploi. Mardi 29 Juin 2004," http://oumma.com/Rentree-2004-mode-d-emploi (accessed July 6, 2008). The compromise scarf is tied in the back of the head and does not cover the neck. Milcent is the author of a book, *Le foulard islamique et la république française: mode d'emploi* (Bobigny: Editions Intégrité, 1995).

18. Bouzar and Kada, *L'une voilée*, 133.

19. Mufti Allie Haroun Sheik, *Morality in Islam: Sexual Issues in Modern Era and Its [sic] Solution in Islam* (New Delhi: Adam, 2008), 86.

20. Chaudhry, *Women's Rights in Islam*, 186.

21. Umm Salamah as-Salafiyyah, *Supporting the Rights of the Believing Women* (Dallas: Tarbiyyah Bookstore Publishing, 2005), 15. The book gives no information about its author. It is introduced by an imam, Muqbil bin Haadee al-Waadi'ee, and provides insight into how a "believing" woman reads injunctions or passages from the Quran as well as the hadith that are problematic for a woman living in a complex world, and interprets them hyperbolically as promoting women's "rights."

22. Sheik, *Morality in Islam*, 91–92. Sheik uses Western sociological and historical theories to make a case for the uniqueness and superiority of Muslim culture regarding women.

23. It is understood that women's presence in the army and the sense of superiority they may experience regarding Muslims of both sexes derive not from their intrinsic worth but from the political and economic structures that empowered women to be accepted into the military as soldiers in the first place.

24. Chaudhry, *Women's Rights in Islam*, 94–95. The author quotes from French sociologist Gustave Le Bon and *Encyclopedia Americana* in defense of polygyny. The same reference to Le Bon appears in Sheik's book, *Morality in Islam*, 106.

25. *Islamic Fatawa Regarding Women*. Shari'a Rulings Given by the Grand Muphti of Saudi Arabia Sheikh Ibn Baz, Sheikh Ibn Uthaimin, Sheikh Ibn Jibreen and Others on Matters Pertaining to Women. Comp. Muhammad bin Abdul-Aziz al-Musnad, trans. Jamaal al-Din M. Zarabozo (Riyadh, Saudi Arabia: Darussalam, 1996), 330, 374, 44.

26. The custom of temporary marriage, legal in Iran, theoretically requires the consent of the parties to it.

27. See Katherine Zoepf, "Saudi King Pardons Rape Victim Sentenced to Be Lashed, Saudi Papers Report," December 18, 2007, http://www.nytimes.com/2007/12/18/world/middleeast/18saudi.html (accessed June 27, 2008).

28. Simona Tersigni uses the expression "groupes allogènes minoritaires" as opposed to "groupes autochtones majoritaires" (or native majority groups) in " 'Prendre le Foulard': les logiques antagoniques de la revendication," *Mouvements*, no. 30 (November–December 2003): 117.

29. It must be noted that Michel Foucault, whose theories have been widely used to sustain this view, had hailed the Iranian Revolution as ushering in a new epistemology. See Janet Afary and Kevin B. Anderson, eds., *Foucault and the Iranian Revolution: Gender and the Seductions of Islamism* (Chicago: University of Chicago Press, 2005).

30. See, among others, Jean-Paul Willaume, "The Cultural Turn in the Sociology of Religion in France," *Sociology of Religion* 65, 4 (2004).

31. See Monica Mookherjee, "Affective Citizenship: Feminism, Postcoloniality and the Politics of Recognition," *Critical Review of International Social and Political Philosophy* 8, 1 (March 2005): 31–50.

32. See my *Eloquence of Silence*, especially the introduction.

33. "Warrior for Al Qaeda Used Internet to Rally Women," *New York Times*, May 28, 2008.

34. Carl Jung defines creed as "a confession of faith intended chiefly for the world at large and is thus an intra-mundane affair, while the meaning and purpose of religion is the relationship of the individual to God (Christianity, Judaism, Islam) or to the path of salvation and liberation (Buddhism)." See *The Undiscovered Self* (New York: Mentor Books, 1958), 31. The organized character of the movement to wear the veil relies on formal entreaties to women that intend to remove the veil from the individual realm of a woman's personal relationship with God. For a discussion that points to the positive conception of women in the Quran,

see Barbara Stowasser, "The Status of Women in Early Islam," in *Muslim Women*, ed. Freda Hussain (New York: St. Martin's Press, 1984); and Azizah al-Hibri, "A Study of Islamic Herstory: Or How Did We Ever Get into This Mess?" in *Women and Islam*, ed. Azizah al-Hibri (New York: Pergamon, 1982).

References

Abou El Fadl, Khaled. *Speaking in God's Name: Islam, Authority and Women*. Oxford: Oneworld, 2001.

Abu-Lughod, Lila. "Do Muslim Women Really Need Saving? Anthropological Reflections on Cultural Relativism and Its Others." *American Anthropologist* 104, 3 (2002): 487–518.

———. *Dramas of Nationhood: The Politics of Television in Egypt*. Chicago: University of Chicago Press, 2005.

Afary, Janet, and Kevin B. Anderson, eds. *Foucault and the Iranian Revolution: Gender and the Seductions of Islamism*. Chicago: University of Chicago Press, 2005.

Al-Hibri, Azizah. "A Study of Islamic Herstory: Or How Did We Ever Get into This Mess?" In *Women and Islam*. Edited by Azizah Al-Hibri. New York: Pergamon, 1982.

Ali, Kecia. *Sexual Ethics and Islam*. Oxford: Oneworld, 2006.

Al-Zo'by, Mazhar, and Khaldoun Samman, eds., *Islam and the Orientalist World System*. London: Enigma Books, 2008.

Amin, Qasim. *The Liberation of Women and the New Woman*. Translated by Samiha Sidhom Peterson. Cairo: American University in Cairo Press, 2004.

Antoun, Richard T. "On the Modesty of Women in Arab Muslim Villages: A Study in the Accommodation of Traditions." *American Anthropologist*, new series 70, 4 (August 1968): 671–97.

As-Salafiyyah, Umm Salamah. *Supporting the Rights of the Believing Women.* Dallas: Tarbiyyah Bookstore Publishing, 2005.

Barlas, Asma. *Believing Women in Islam: Unreading Patriarchal Interpretations of the Qur'an.* Austin: University of Texas Press, 2002.

Bisiaux, Marcel and Catherine Jajolet. *A ma mère: 50 écrivains parlent de leur mère.* Paris: Pierre Horay, 1988–2006.

Boubekeur, Amel. "Female Religious Professionals in France." *ISIM Newsletter,* no. 14 (June 2004).

———. "Modernité des jeunes filles voilées." *CERAS Projet, Recherche et Action Sociales,* no. 287 (July 2005). http://www.ceras-projet.com/index.php?id=1134 (accessed November 11, 2007).

Bouzar, Dounia. *L'Islam des banlieues, les prédicateurs musulmans, nouveaux travailleurs sociaux?* Paris: Syros-La Découverte, 2001.

Bouzar, Dounia, and Saïda Kada. *L'une voilée, l'autre pas.* Paris: Albin Michel, 2003.

Brenner, Susan. "Reconstructing Self and Society: Javanese Muslim Women." *American Ethnologist* 23, 4 (1996): 673–97.

Bullock, Katherine. *Rethinking Muslim Women and the Veil: Challenging Historical and Modern Stereotypes.* Herndon, VA: International Institute of Islamic Thought, 2003.

Chaudhary, Ajay Singh. "'The Simulacra of Morality': Islamic Veiling, Religious Politics and the Limits of Liberalism." *Dialectical Anthropology* 29 (2005): 349–72.

Chaudhry, Muhammad Sharif. *Women's Rights in Islam.* New Delhi: Adam, 2008.

Choudhury, Nusrat. "From the Stasi Commission to the European Court of Human Rights: *L'Affaire du Foulard* and the Challenge of Protecting the Rights of Muslim Girls." *Columbia Journal of Gender and Law* 16 (January 2007): 199–290.

Djitli, Leïla. *Lettre à ma fille qui veut porter le voile.* Lonrai, Normandie: Doc en Stock/Editions de la Martinière, 2004.

Driver, Julia. "Modesty and Ignorance." *Ethics* 109, 4 (July 1999): 827–34.

El Guindi, Fadwa. *Veil: Modesty, Privacy and Resistance.* Oxford: Berg, 1999.

Fregosi, Frank. "Champs religieux official et contre-champ islamique." In *La politisation du voile*. Edited by Françoise Lorcerie. Paris: L'Harmattan, 2005.

Göler, Nilüfer. *The Forbidden Modern: Civilization and Veiling*. Ann Arbor: University of Michigan Press, 1996.

———. "The Voluntary Adoption of Islamic Stigma Symbols." *Social Research* 70, 3 (Fall 2003): 809–28.

Halimi, Gisèle. "Laïcité: une loi pour la cohésion. 23 Octobre 2003." http://www.sisyphe.org/article.php3?id_article=730 (accessed December 11, 2007).

Hessini, Leila. "Wearing the Hijab in Contemporary Morocco: Choice and Identity." In *Reconstructing Gender in the Middle East: Tradition, Identity and Power*. Edited by Fatma Müge Göçek and Shiva Balaghi. New York: Columbia University Press, 1994, 40–56.

Hoodfar, Homa, "Return to the Veil: Personal Strategies and Public Participation in Egypt." In *Working Women: International Perspectives on Labor and Gender Ideology*. Edited by Nanneke Redclift and M. Thea Sinclair. London: Routledge, 1991, 104–24.

Hooker, M. D. "Authority on her Head: An Examination of I COR. XI.10." *New Testament Studies* 10 (October 1963): 410–16.

Islamic Fatawa Regarding Women. Shari'a Rulings Given by the Grand Muphti of Saudi Arabia Sheikh Ibn Baz, Sheikh Ibn Uthaimin, Sheikh Ibn Jibreen and Others on Matters Pertaining to Women. Compiled by Muhammad bin Abdul-Aziz Al-Musnad, translated by Jamaal al-Din M. Zarabozo. Riyadh, Saudi Arabia: Darussalam, 1996.

Jaubert, Annie. "Le voile des femmes (I COR. XI.2–16)." *New Testament Studies* 18 (October 1972): 419–30.

Jung, C. G. *The Undiscovered Self*. New York: Mentor Books, 1958.

Karam, Azza. *Women, Islamisms and the State: Contemporary Feminisms in Egypt*. New York: St. Martin's, 1998.

Keddie, Nikki R. *An Islamic Response to Imperialism: Political and Religious Writings of Sayyid Jamal ad-Din "al Afghani."* Berkeley: University of California Press, 1968.

Keddie, Nikki R. *Women in the Middle East: Past and Present.* Princeton: Princeton University Press, 2007.

Killian, Caitlin, and Cathryn Johnson, "'I Am Not an Immigrant!' Resistance, Redefinition, and the Role of Resources in Identity Work." *Social Psychological Quarterly* 69, 1 (2006): 60–80.

Koppelman, Connie. "The Politics of Hair." *Frontiers: A Journal of Women's Studies* 17, 2 (1996): 87–88.

Lazreg, Marnia. "Consequences of Political Liberalization and Socio-Cultural Mobilization for Women in Algeria, Egypt and Jordan." In *Governing Women: Women's Political Effectiveness in Contexts of Democratization and Governance Reform.* Edited by Anne-Marie Goetz. New York: Routledge, 2009, 45–62.

———. *The Eloquence of Silence: Algerian Women in Question.* New York: Routledge, 1994.

———. *Torture and the Twilight of Empire: From Algiers to Baghdad.* Princeton: Princeton University Press, 2008.

Leonetti, Taboada Isabel. *Les Femmes et l' Islam. Entre modernité et intégrisme.* Paris: L'Harmattan, 2004.

Lorcerie, Françoise, ed. *La politicization du voile en France, en Europe et dans le monde arabe.* Paris: L'Harmattan, 2005.

MacLeod, Arlene Elowe. *Accommodating Protest: Working Women, the New Veil and Change in Cairo.* New York: Columbia University Press, 1991.

Mahmood, Saba. *Politics of Piety: The Islamic Revival and the Feminist Subject.* Princeton: Princeton University Press, 2005.

Mernissi, Fatima. *The Veil and the Male Elite.* Reading, MA: Perseus Books, 1991.

Michel, Patrick. "Espace ouvert, identités plurielles: les recompositions contemporaines du croire." *Social Compass* 53, 2 (2006): 227–41.

Moazzam, Anwar. *Jamal al-Din al-Afghani: A Muslim Intellectual.* New Delhi: Concept, 1984.

Mookherjee, Monica. "Affective Citizenship: Feminism, Postcoloniality and the Politics of Recognition." *Critical Review of International Social and Political Philosophy* 8, 1 (March 2005): 31–50.

Morgan, Elizabeth. "Mary and Modesty." *Christianity and Literature* 54, 2 (Winter 2005): 209–33.

Mule, Pat, and Diane Barthel. "The Return to the Veil: Individual Autonomy vs. Social Esteem." *Sociological Forum* 7, 2 (June 1994): 323–32.

Najmabadi, Afsaneh. "Veiled Discourse—Unveiled Bodies." *Feminist Studies* 19, 3 (Autumn 1993): 487–518.

Ramadan, Tariq. *Western Muslims and the Future of Islam*. Oxford: Oxford University Press, 2004.

Sahih Al-Bukhari Summarized. Arabic–English. Compiled by Al-Imam Zain-ud-Din Ahmad bin Abdul-Lateef Az-Zubaidi, translated by Muhammad Muhsin Khan. Riyadh, Saudi Arabia: Maktaba Darussalam, 1996.

Sarwar, Ghulam. *Islam: Beliefs and Teachings*. Revised edition. New Delhi: Markazi Maktaba Islami, 2000.

Schueler, G. F. "Why Modesty Is a Virtue. *Ethics* 107, 3 (April 1997): 467–85.

Scott, Joan Wallach. *The Politics of the Veil*. Princeton: Princeton University Press, 2007.

Sheik, Mufti Allie Haroun. *Morality in Islam: Sexual Issues in Modern Era and Its [sic] Solution in Islam*. New Delhi: Adam, 2008.

Shirazi, Faegheh. *The Veil Unveiled: The Hijab in Modern Culture*. Gainesville: University Press of Florida, 2001.

Stowasser, Barbara. "The Status of Women in Early Islam." In *Muslim Women*. Edited by Freda Hussain. New York: St. Martin's Press, 1984.

Tersigni, Simona. "'Prendre le Foulard': les logiques antagoniques de la revendication." *Mouvements*, no. 30 (November–December 2003): 116–22.

Wadud, Amina. *Inside the Gender Jihad: Women's Reform in Islam*. Oxford: One World, 2006.

Willaume, Jean-Paul. "The Cultural Turn in the Sociology of Religion in France." *Sociology of Religion* 65, 4 (2004).

Zuhur, Sherifa. *Revealing Reveiling: Islamist Ideology in Contemporary Egypt*. Albany: State University of New York Press, 1992.

Index